GET ON BOARD
The Story of the
Underground Railroad

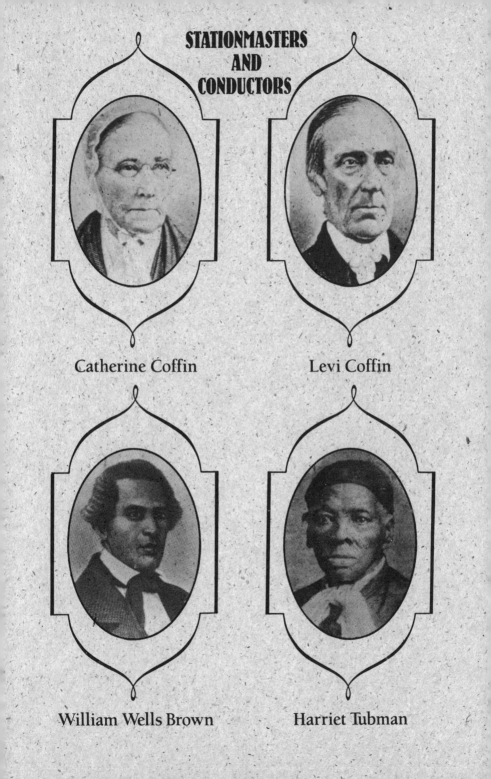

STATIONMASTERS AND CONDUCTORS

Catherine Coffin

Levi Coffin

William Wells Brown

Harriet Tubman

GET ON BOARD
The Story of the
Underground Railroad

SCHOLASTIC
HARDCOVER

Scholastic Inc.
New York

Library of Congress Cataloging-in-Publication Data

Haskins, James, 1941–
   Get on board : the story of the Underground Railroad / by Jim
Haskins.
      p.   cm.
Includes bibliographical references and index.
Summary: Discusses the Underground Railroad, the secret, loosely
organized network of people and places that helped many slaves
escape north to freedom.

ISBN 0-590-45418-8

   1. Underground railroad — Juvenile literature.   2. Fugitive slaves —
United States — History — 19th century — Juvenile literature.
[1. Underground railroad.   2. Fugitive slaves.]   I. Title.
                     E450.H315   1993
                     973.7'115 — dc20
                        92-13247
                           CIP
                           AC

12 11 10 9 8 7 6 5 4 3 2 1   3 4 5 6 7 8/9

First Scholastic printing, January 1993

Acknowledgments

*I am grateful to Kathy Benson,
Deborah C. Brudno, and
Ann Kalkhoff, for their help.*

To Louise Stephenson

Contents

THE UNDERGROUND RAIL ROAD

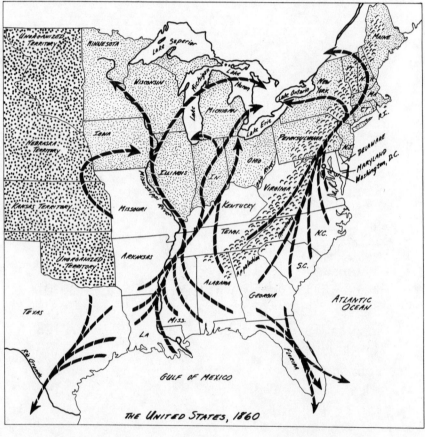

THE UNITED STATES, 1860

1

How the Underground Railroad Got Its Name

There is a story in Underground Railroad lore that in 1831 a slave named Tice Davids ran away from his master in Kentucky. With the master in hot pursuit, Davids made his way to the Ohio River, which formed the border between the slave state of Kentucky and the free state of Ohio. The master saw Davids plunge into the river and, as he searched frantically for a boat, kept his eyes on his slave. When he set off after his slave in a boat, he went directly toward him. When Davids reached the opposite shore near the town of Ripley, Ohio, his master was just minutes behind him. But then Tice Davids vanished from sight.

The owner combed the countryside. He searched through Ripley, which was known as an anti-slavery town. But he could find no trace of his runaway slave. He finally gave up, concluding that Davids had escaped on "an underground road."

The story spread about the slave who had gained his freedom on an "underground road." As it spread, it was added to, as stories often are. Steam-engine railroad trains had just come into use. The *Tom Thumb*, a steam-powered locomotive built by Peter Cooper, had its first successful run in 1830. The changeover from horse-drawn engines to steam-powered ones inaugurated the great age of the railroad that still excites peoples' imaginations. Pretty soon the story was that Tice Davids had escaped on an *underground railroad*.

There never was an actual railroad that ran underground and carried escaped slaves to freedom. But the term fit the way many slaves in the South made their way to the free states of the North and even to Canada, for they always traveled in secret, or "underground." The term "underground railroad" first appeared in print in the 1840s, and soon other railroad terms were being used. The fugitive slaves were referred to as "parcels" and "passengers." Those who helped them in one way or another along the way were called "conductors." People who offered their homes as "depots" or "stations" were called "stationmasters."

No one knows who helped the slave named Tice Davids — if indeed there ever was a real Tice Davids. His story may be a myth, for there is at least

A slave escapes on horseback.

one other version of the origin of the term "underground railroad" that places its beginning in Chester
County, Pennsylvania. No one knows whether Tice
Davids, if he was a real person, succeeded in reaching
a place where he could live in freedom. No one
knows how many slaves tried to escape, or how many
people tried to help them during the two-and-a-half
centuries of slavery in the United States.

Especially in the early days, the Underground
Railroad was a secret activity, and few written records were kept. The names of most of the slaves who
escaped, and the names of many people — black and
white — who aided them, are lost to history. But
hundreds of stories have survived, and altogether
they make a thrilling chapter in the long history of
slavery and the attempts to fight it.

2
A Long History of Slave Escapes, and of Fugitive Slave Laws

From the time the New World African slave trade began, men and women in bondage tried to escape. African men and women being transported on ships from the West Coast of Africa committed suicide by jumping overboard or refusing to eat, rather than allow themselves to be taken to an unknown land and a life of bondage. Some groups of slaves aboard slave ships managed to revolt and overpower the crew. The most famous shipboard slave revolt occurred in 1839 on the Spanish slave ship *Amistad* bound for Cuba. Led by Joseph Cinque, the son of an African king, fifty-three Africans seized the ship and ordered a handful of crewmen to sail back to Africa. But the sailors tricked the Africans and headed instead for the coast of North America.

Joseph Cinque and his men were captured off Long Island.

Bringing slaves directly from Africa was illegal in the United States by 1839. But slaves could still be gotten from the Caribbean, and slavery was still legal. Some Americans believed that the Africans of the *Amistad* should be allowed to return to their homeland. Others, not wanting to anger Spain, argued that the slaves on the *Amistad* should be handed over to Spanish authorities. John Quincy Adams, a former president of the United States, represented the Africans in a case that went all the way to the United States Supreme Court, which ruled that the men should be allowed to go free. Eventually, they were returned to Africa.

Once slaves reached American shores, they continued to fight against the yoke of bondage by planning and carrying out revolts. Most of these revolts were put down and the slaves killed. More successful were the instances of individual or small-group slave escapes, especially when the slaves did not have to travel far to reach freedom.

The first American to die in the cause of the American Revolution was a fugitive slave named Crispus Attucks. Born into slavery, probably in the colony of Massachusetts, by 1750 he was the property of a William Brown of Framingham, Massachusetts. On October 2, 1750, Brown ran an ad in the *Boston Gazette* offering a reward of ten pounds for the return of his slave, warning "allMasters of Vessels and oth-

RAN-away from his Master *William Brown* of *Framingham*, on the 30th of *Sept.* last, a Molatto Fellow, about 27 Years of Age, named *Crispas*, 6 Feet twoInches high, short curl'd Hair, his Knees nearer together than common; had on a light colour'd Bearskin Coat, plain brown Fustian Jacket, or brown all-Wool one, new Buckskin Breeches, blue YarnStockings, and a check'd woollenShirt. Whoever shall take up said Run-away, and convey him to his abovesaidMaster, shall have *ten Pounds*, old TenorReward, and all necessary Charges paid. And allMasters of Vessels and others, are hereby caution'd against concealing or carrying off saidServant onPenalty of the Law. *Boston, October* 2. 1750.

An ad from the Boston Gazette, October 2, 1750, requesting the capture of Crispus Attucks, a runaway who later became the first American to die in the Revolution.

ers, are hereby caution'd against concealing or carrying off saidServant on Penalty of the Law."

Many blacks, slave and free, worked on ships out of, or on the docks in, the port cities along the North American coast. A fugitive slave like Attucks could escape detection by blending in with other blacks in the shipping industry. Attucks managed to remain at large for twenty years, probably working on cargo ships that sailed to and from the West Indies, and on whaling ships off the New England coast, until he was killed in a battle in 1770 between colonists and British troops in Boston. That battle came to be called the Boston Massacre.

Native Americans helped harbor escaped slaves. Slaves in both the North and the South were taken in by local Indian tribes and often spent the rest of their lives living with Native Americans. The Seminole Indians of Florida are among the tribes who welcomed and intermarried with escaped slaves.

Off the coast of South Carolina and Georgia are a number of islands, called sea islands, that were a natural destination for escaped slaves, who could disappear into their remote reaches and evade capture. On certain of these sea islands off South Carolina, escaped slaves and their descendants evolved a whole culture, called Geechee, that continued many African language patterns and traditions long after they had disappeared in the mainland slave population.

Far more difficult and dangerous was escape from the South to the North. Most southern slaves had never been to the North and had only a vague idea where it was. Slaveholding states had laws forbidding the education of slaves, and so they could not read about the North. They had to depend on what they could overhear in the master's house, or on stories whispered in the slave quarters. Sometimes all they knew was that if they followed the North Star at the end of the Little Dipper they would eventually reach free territory. That knowledge did them no good on cloudy, starless nights, but they also knew that moss only grows on the north side of trees, so they could continue on their perilous journey. Still, they faced many obstacles.

Runaway slaves risked discovery and capture all along the way. There were slave hunters who earned their living tracking and bringing back escaped slaves in exchange for the rewards slave owners were willing to pay for the return of their valuable property. Local sheriffs, other slave masters, and people who supported slavery, or simply believed they should obey the fugitive slave laws, were always on the lookout for runaways. Thus, runaways had to stay away from populated centers and public roads, especially during the day. They traveled mostly at night, spending days hiding out in swamps and forests and fields, often owning nothing but the clothes on their backs.

This illustration depicts an escaped slave hiding out in the woods.

They suffered from exposure to cold and rain. What little food they were able to take with them, they ate in a matter of days, and often had to continue their journey weak with hunger. Many must have died on the unbroken trails they had to blaze for themselves across mountains and rivers and through forests and swamps. There were no well-worn routes for them to follow, and those slaves who did make it to safety did not dare to return to tell others how to get there.

But for the slaves who had the courage to run away, the dream of freedom was more powerful than the suffering they had to undergo to escape bondage. And kind and principled people helped the fortunate ones to realize their dream.

By the end of the Revolutionary War, the first attempts to aid fugitives in an organized fashion were taking shape. In 1786, George Washington complained that "a society of Quakers, formed for such purposes, have attempted to liberate" one of his slaves, who had escaped from Alexandria, Virginia, to Philadelphia.

The following year, a Quaker teenager named Isaac T. Hopper, who had settled in Philadelphia, began to organize a system for hiding and aiding fugitive slaves. Within a few years, escaped slaves were being helped in a number of towns in Pennsylvania and New Jersey.

Even before the birth of the United States, slaveholders were concerned about losing their slaves, and

Isaac T. Hopper, a pioneer in the Underground Railroad movement, assisted runaways traveling through New York.

about the help fugitives were getting from non-slaveholders. A clause concerning the problem of fugitive slaves was included in the United States Constitution. Representatives of the slaveholding former colonies insisted on it. The Revolutionary War had disrupted the southern economy. Slaveholders wanted to get back to business as soon as they could, and they wanted to make sure their slaves were around to do the work. That meant giving the owners a legal basis for retrieving the slaves who fled to free states.

Introduced and adopted at the Philadelphia Convention of 1787, Article IV, clause 2 of the Constitution became known as the "fugitive slave and felon clause" and read in part:

No person held to service or labor in one state, under the laws thereof, escaping into another, shall, in consequence of any law or regulation therein, be discharged from such service or labor, but shall be delivered up on claim of the party to whom such service or labor may be due.

Although the word *slave* was never used, just as it was not used anywhere else in the Constitution, the meaning of the clause was clear: Any slave who fled a slave state to a free state had to be returned to his or her owner.

Soon, however, it became evident that the law had to be even clearer about the issue of fugitive slaves and a penalty had to be provided for helping

Many runaways, and even free blacks, found themselves enslaved under the Fugitive Slave Law, which empowered slaveholders to reclaim their "property," above and below the Mason Dixon line.

them. Many free states paid little attention to the clause and refused to help slave owners get back their property. The slave states pushed for a law specifically aimed at the free-state citizens who helped runaways. The first Fugitive Slave Act was passed by Congress in Philadelphia, then the capital of the United States, in 1793. The act made it a crime to help an escaped slave or prevent his or her arrest.

But many state and local governments in the free states paid no attention to the federal law. In 1804, General Thomas Boude, an officer during the Revolutionary War, bought a slave named Stephen Smith and took him home to Columbia, Pennsylvania. Soon afterward, Smith's mother escaped and followed her son to Columbia, where Boude took her in. When the owner of Smith's mother arrived to demand her property, Boude refused to surrender her, and the people of Columbia supported him. In fact, the townspeople decided to do all they could to help other fugitives.

Meanwhile, people in Ohio, just across the Ohio River from the slave state of Kentucky, were doing the same.

As a result of the first fugitive slave law, Canada became an important destination for escaped slaves, who could not feel entirely safe anywhere in the United States. By 1826 there were so many fugitive slaves living in Canada that plantation owners in Maryland and Kentucky asked United States Secretary of State Henry Clay to work out a plan with

Jarmain Wesley Loguen was known as the "Underground Railroad King."

the Canadian government under which escaped slaves could be lawfully returned to their owners. Clay wrote to the Canadian government and waited impatiently for a reply. When it came, he was disappointed. The Canadian government offered no help in returning the escaped slaves who were living within its borders.

Canada was hundreds of miles from the slave states, and it was a long, perilous journey to reach her borders. Even so, for those slaves whose dream of freedom outweighed all other considerations, there were people who helped them along the way. And as time went on, those people became organized into the network that came to be called the Underground Railroad.

3
The Tracks
and Stations

The formal Underground Railroad was not really organized until the early 1830s. It was primarily a northern activity, covering an area generally above the Ohio River in the Midwest, along the state line of Pennsylvania in the East, and stretching into Canada. There are maps of Underground Railroad routes that show heavy activity in Illinois, Indiana, Ohio, Pennsylvania, Delaware, and the New England states. Over time, however, the term Underground Railroad has come to apply in general to the routes escaped slaves took to the North and freedom.

A map of Underground Railroad routes was published in 1898 in a book entitled *The Underground Railroad: From Slavery to Freedom* by Wilbur H. Siebert. It shows a maze of lines from the borders of Missouri, Kentucky, West Virginia, and Pennsylvania northward to Canada. In a small state like Delaware, the lines are so thick it is difficult to distinguish them. Indiana, Ohio, and Illinois had several concentrated areas of Underground Railroad routes, as did western Pennsylvania and New York.

Siebert also provided a detailed map of routes in "Chester and the Neighboring Counties of Pennsylvania." He even included the names of some stationmasters, among them J. N. Russell and Thomas Whitson, Oliver Furness, and John Vickers.

One of the main routes through Michigan started in Cass County and went through Cassopolis, Schoolcraft, Climax, Battle Creek, Marshall, Albion, Jackson, and other towns along the route of the Michigan Central Railroad. The stations were usually between ten and twenty miles apart, with the average distance being about twelve miles. That was the distance a healthy man could travel on foot, or a wagon carrying several slaves could cover at night, for travel from place to place occurred only at night except in grave emergencies. Sometimes at Detroit, and sometimes farther north, the fugitive slaves could be ferried across the Detroit River into Canada.

The New England states were also important in the Underground Railroad. Many fugitives who reached the eastern part of New York State continued on up through Connecticut, and from there

Thomas Whitson and his sister Leah C. Smith, stationmasters in Chester County, Pennsylvania.

through Massachusetts or Vermont. The port cities of Providence, Rhode Island, and Boston, Massachusetts, were often the destinations of fugitives traveling by boat from Norfolk and Portsmouth, Virginia. From these ports, they continued their journey overland to Canada.

Water transportation was used on inland routes as well. In Vermont, at Castleton, near Rutland, Erastus and Harvey O. Higley welcomed fugitives and guided them to Fair Haven, where Zenas C. Ellis hid them in his fishing boats and transported them to Whitehall. There, they boarded canal boats heading for Canada on the Champlain Canal.

The stations were as varied as the routes. They included attics, barns, and potato cellars, not to mention secret rooms, fake closets, trapdoors, and hidden tunnels. Josiah B. Grinnell of Iowa had a secret chamber he called the "liberty room."

The Tallman house in Janesville, Wisconsin, was built for the purpose of hiding many fugitives. Built between 1855 and 1857, it was made of brick and had twenty rooms. There were hiding places in both the basement and the attic, and a special lookout on the roof. Runaway slaves entered by the cellar door, which was always left open. When it was time to leave, the fugitives were led through a secret stairway in a maid's closet and through an underground tunnel leading to the Rock River. From there, they were taken by riverboat to the town of Milton.

In Milton was the Stage Coach Inn, operated by

Josiah B. Grinell and his wife
sheltered dozens of runaways
in their home.

Joshua Goodrich. He dug a tunnel between his inn and a log cabin some yards away. Fugitives were led to the cabin, whose floor had a secret trapdoor. The trapdoor led to the tunnel, at the end of which was a secret hiding place in the basement of the inn.

In the early days of the Underground Railroad, most of the fugitives were men, and they usually traveled on foot. In later years, as the number of fugitives increased, and "passengers" included women and children, wagons and drivers were used to transport them from one place to another. Many Underground Railroad agents simply covered the people in the wagons with blankets. Others built secret compartments beneath false bottoms. The slaves lay down in the secret compartments and were

This illustration shows the false bottom of a wooden wagon used to transport runaways from station to station on the Underground Railroad.

covered by the floorboards of the false bottoms. Then hay or vegetables were piled upon the floorboards.

Special signs or signals often helped fugitives or agents find an Underground Railroad station. Sometimes the signal was a barn lantern with a special colored shade. The signs had to be visible at night. In parts of Vermont, a chimney with a row of white-painted bricks was a sign that the household welcomed fugitives. In Ohio, a woman named Mrs. Piatt put a flag in the hand of a small statue in front of her house when fugitives were welcome. When the statue held no flag, runaways had to continue on until they found another station.

Usually once a conductor, or a fugitive, identified a station he or she would knock at the door and, when asked who it was would answer, "A friend with friends."

4
The Stationmasters

In his book about the Underground Railroad, published in 1898, Wilbur H. Siebert recorded more than thirty-two hundred active workers. There is no way to estimate how many were never identified or what their race was, but it is likely that many of the anonymous stationmasters were black.

Free blacks were an important source of help for escaped slaves. In fact, in the early days before whites in significant numbers began to help runaways, free blacks were more likely to help than were whites, whom escaped slaves would not have trusted to aid them. Even after whites began to help in an organized fashion, blacks who had already escaped reached back to help those who were still enslaved. In fact, the story of the Underground Railroad that has come down through history tends to understate the role of free blacks. One reason may be that more records were kept by whites. Another is that white contributions to American history have been written about for a longer time and more frequently than important contributions by blacks.

Among the well-known black stationmasters on the Underground Railroad was Jarmain Wesley Loguen, who was a fugitive slave himself. Owned by Manasseth and Sarah Logue in Maury County, Tennessee, he had escaped and reached Canada. He later settled near Syracuse, New York. As a free man, he took the last name Loguen, adding one letter to the end of the name of his master. He became a minister and, with his wife, Caroline, established two Un-

Jarmain Wesley Loguen, known as the "Underground Railroad King," settled in Syracuse, New York, where he served as a minister and stationmaster on the Underground Railroad.

Helen Amelia, Loguen's daughter, assisted her father with the operations of two Underground Railroad stations in Syracuse.

derground Railroad stations in Syracuse: one at their home and one at his church. Credited with helping some fifteen hundred fugitive slaves reach Canada, he was known as the "Underground Railroad King."

Loguen was close friends with Harriet Tubman, known as Moses because of the hundreds of escaped slaves she conducted to freedom. He welcomed her and her fugitive charges whenever she came his way. He also supported John Brown, a white man who in 1859 tried and failed to rescue hundreds of slaves in Virginia by arming them with guns and ammunition from a captured government arsenal.

Also in 1859, his narrative *The Rev. J.W. Loguen, as a Slave and as a Freeman*, was published. Probably as the result of the publication, Loguen's former mistress in Tennessee learned where he was. In February 1860 she wrote to "Jarm." Here is part of her letter:

. . . I write you these lines to let you know the situation we are in — partly in consequence of your running away and stealing Old Rock, our fine mare. . . . I am cripple, but I am still able to get about. The rest of the family are all well. . . . Though we got the mare back, she was never worth much after you took her, and, as I now stand in need of some funds, I am determined to sell you. If you will send me one thousand dollars and pay for the old mare I will give up all claim I have to you. . . .

In consequence of your running away, we had to sell Abe and Ann and twelve acres of land; and I want you to send me the money that I may be able to redeem the land that you was the cause of our selling, and on receipt of the above named sum of money, I will send you your bill of sale. If you do not comply with my request, I will sell you to some one else. . . .

I understand that you are a preacher. . . . I would like to know if you read your Bible? If so, can you tell what will become of the thief if he does not repent? . . . You know that we reared you as we reared our own children; that you was never abused, and that shortly before you ran away, when your master asked you if you would like to be sold, you said you would not leave him to go with any body.

Here is part of the letter Loguen wrote in response to "Mrs. Sarah Logue":

. . . You sold my brother and sister, Abe and Ann, and twelve acres of land, you say, because I ran away. Now you have the unutterable meanness to ask me to return and be your miserable chattel, or in lieu thereof send you one thousand dollars to enable you to redeem the *land*, but not to redeem my poor brother and sister! . . .

You say, 'You know we raised you as we did our own children?' Woman, did you raise your *own children* for the market? Did you raise them for the whipping post? Did you raise them to be drove off in a coffle in chains? Where are my poor bleeding brothers and sisters? Can you tell? Who was it that sent them off into sugar and cotton fields, to be kicked, and cuffed, and whipped, and to groan and die; and where no kin can hear their groans, or attend and sympathize at their dying bed, or follow in their funeral?

. . . You say I am a thief, because I took the old mare along with me. Have you got to learn that I had a better right to the old mare, as you call her, than *Manasseth Logue* had to me? Is it a greater sin for me to steal his horse, than it was for him to rob my mother's cradle and steal me? . . . Before God

and High Heaven, is there a law for one man which
is not law for every other man?

. . . Do you think to terrify me by presenting the
alternative to give my money to you, or give my
body to Slavery? . . . I stand among a free people,
who, I thank God, sympathize with my rights, and
the rights of mankind; and if your emissaries and
venders come here, to re-enslave me, and escape the
unshrinking vigor of my own right arm, I trust my
strong and brave friends, in this City and State, will
be my rescuers and avengers.

The most famous former fugitive slave, Frederick
Douglass, was also a stationmaster, although he
did not engage in that activity full time. Rather,
his and his wife Anne's home in Rochester, New
York, was what was called an "overflow" station:
When other stations in Rochester could not accept
any more fugitives, the Douglasses would welcome
them.

While living in Rochester, Douglass published a
newspaper called *North Star*. The very first issue in
1847 stated that its editor was involved in the Underground Railroad. Harriet Tubman brought fugitives to the Douglass home on several occasions,
probably including the time she conducted a party
of eleven people to Canada. According to Douglass,
the largest group he'd ever sheltered numbered
eleven. He added that "it was difficult for me to give
shelter, food, and money for so many at once, but

Anna Murray Douglass, wife of Frederick Douglass, helped runaways escape. Their home in Syracuse, New York, served as an "overflow" station.

Frederick Douglass not only served as a stationmaster but also lectured and edited a newspaper all for the cause of the abolition of slavery.

Underground railroad pass signed by Frederick Douglass, which reads: "My Dear Mrs. Post: Please shelter this Sister from the house of bondage till five o'clock — this afternoon — She will then be sent on to the land of freedom. Yours truly, Fred K."

it had to be done so they could be moved on immediately to Canada."

Among white stationmasters, the Quakers were the earliest and most well-known and organized group. They were formally known as the Religious Society of Friends, and they originated the Underground Railroad announcement that passengers had arrived at a station: "A friend with friends."

Founded in England in the middle of the seventeenth century, the Quakers got their nickname from those who mocked them. Their founder, George Fox, told them to "tremble at the word of the Lord." Quake is another word for tremble. Members of the Religious Society of Friends believed in the equality of all men and women, opposed war, and regarded the rituals of the church as unimportant to Christian life.

Quakers were persecuted in England, and many emigrated to the New World seeking religious freedom. The colony of Pennsylvania was established in 1682 by William Penn, a Quaker, as a haven for all Quakers. There was complete freedom of worship in Pennsylvania, as there was in Rhode Island. In other colonies, Quakers were sometimes persecuted.

Some Quakers felt that belief in the quality of all people meant working against slavery and on behalf of fugitive slaves. But not all felt that way. There were Societies of Friends that refused to admit black members and that shunned those white members in their midst who worked in the Underground Railroad. But enough Quakers did take part in the anti-slavery cause to become a legendary part of the Underground Railroad.

The work of Thomas Garrett has been well documented. Born in Pennsylvania in 1789, Garrett settled in Wilmington, Delaware, in 1822, where he began offering food and shelter to runaway slaves and doing whatever he could to aid them. It is estimated that some 2,500 fugitive slaves passed through his home, and that these included groups of slaves being shepherded by Harriet Tubman, the most famous "conductor" on the Underground Railroad.

In 1848, after he helped a man transport his enslaved family from Wilmington to Philadelphia, Gar-

Thomas Garrett, a Pennsylvania born Quaker, became one of the principal organizers of the Underground Railroad in the Mid-Atlantic region.

rett was arrested, tried, and found guilty of breaking the fugitive slave law. The fine of five thousand dollars took all the money he had, and also forced him to sell his belongings at public auction to pay the fine. The sheriff who conducted the sale said to Garrett, "Thomas, I hope you'll never be caught at this again," whereupon Garrett replied, "Friend, I haven't a dollar in the world, but if thee knows a fugitive anywhere on the face of the earth who needs a breakfast, send him to me."

The Coffin family were also important Underground Railroad stationmasters. Vestal Coffin is reported to have organized a system of aiding fugitives in North Carolina in 1819, and his son, Addison, followed in his footsteps. Vestal's cousin, Levi, also helped out during the years he lived in North Carolina. Writing about those years, Levi Coffin recalled,

> Runaway slaves used frequently to conceal themselves in the woods and thickets of New Garden, waiting opportunities to make their escape to the North, and I generally learned their places of concealment and rendered them all the service in my power. These outlying slaves knew where I lived, and, when reduced to extremity of want or danger, often came to my room, in the silence and darkness of the night, to obtain food or assistance.

After Levi moved to Indiana in 1826 and opened a store, he set up an Underground Railroad network around Newport (later called Fountain City) on the East Fork of the Ohio River above Cincinnati, Ohio. His and his wife Catherine's two-story, red-brick house had a basement that was used as a hiding place. His barn held a horse and wagon ready to go. Over time, three different lines on the Underground Railroad converged on the Coffin home.

In 1876, Coffin's *Reminiscence* was published. In it, he described a typical arrival of fugitives at his door:

> We knew not what night or what hour of the night we would be roused from slumber by a

The famous red brick house of Levi and Catherine Coffin is reputed to have harbored thousands of runaways escaping through Fountain City, Indiana.

gentle rap at the door. . . . I have often been awakened by this signal, and sprang out of bed in the dark and opened the door. Outside in the cold or rain, there would be a two-horse wagon loaded with fugitives, perhaps the greater part of them women and children. I would invite them, in a low tone, to come in, and they would follow me into the house without a word, for we knew not who might be watching and listening. When they were all safely inside and the door fastened, I would cover the windows, strike a light and build a good fire. By this time my wife would be up and preparing victuals for them, and in a short time the cold and hungry fugitives would be made comfortable . . . The fugitives would rest on pallets before the fire the rest of the night. Frequently, wagon-loads of passengers from the different lines have met at our house, having no previous knowledge of each other. The companies varied in number, from two or three fugitives to seventeen. . . .

Coffin was sometimes called the "President" of the Underground Railroad.

5
The Conductors

Conductors sometimes traveled short distances and sometimes very long distances with fugitive slaves. A conductor could be a wagon driver who drove a wagonload of slaves twelve miles or a steamboat worker who hid slave stowaways. A conductor could also be someone who traveled to the South to spread the word to slaves that they could escape to freedom and to give them directions. Some even personally led them to freedom. That type of conducting was one of the most dangerous jobs on the Underground Railroad.

There were several famous white conductors. One was Calvin Fairbanks, who had come to hate slavery while he was a student at Oberlin College in Ohio. In 1837 he began to travel south into Kentucky to help free slaves, and he regularly transported fugitives across the Ohio River. While in Kentucky, he became friendly with a schoolteacher from Vermont named Delia Webster, who agreed to help him. But they were discovered and arrested. She was released and allowed to return to Vermont, but he was imprisoned. Pardoned in 1849, after serving five years, Fairbanks went right back to the business of aiding slaves to escape from Kentucky.

John Fairfield was born into a slaveholding family in Virginia and played with slave children when he was young. Many young whites did the same, but later saw nothing wrong with the idea that they were free while their childhood friends were slaves. When Fairfield was old enough to leave home, he decided to leave the slave states altogether and settle in Ohio. He also decided to take with him a slave named Bill who belonged to his uncle and who had been Fairfield's friend since they were children.

The two made secret plans, and on the night Fairfield left for Ohio, Bill stole one of his master's horses and met him at a previously arranged place. The two then traveled to Ohio as master and slave. From Ohio, Fairfield accompanied Bill to Canada and stayed there until Bill was settled.

Fairfield then went back to Ohio and spent several months there before he returned to Virginia. Back home, he learned that his uncle suspected him of helping Bill escape and planned to have him arrested. Fairfield decided to leave Ohio, this time

KENTUCKY JURSIPRUDENCE.

A HISTORY OF THE TRIAL OF

MISS DELIA A. WEBSTER.

At Lexington, Kentucky, Dec'r 17-21, 1844,

BEFORE THE HON. RICHARD BUCKNER.

ON A CHARGE OF AIDING SLAVES TO ESCAPE FROM
THAT COMMONWEALTH—WITH MISCELLANEOUS REMARKS
INCLUDING HER VIEWS ON AMERICAN SLAVERY.

WRITTEN BY HERSELF.

" HE THAT FILCHES FROM ME MY GOOD NAME
ROBS ME OF THAT WHICH NOT ENRICHETH HIM,
AND MAKES ME POOR INDEED " —*Shakspeare's Othello*

~~~~~~~~~~~~~

VERGENNES:

E. W. BLAISDELL, PRINTER.

1845.

Title page from A History of the Trial of Miss Delia A. Webster, *a schoolteacher who was arrested along with Calvin Fairbanks for aiding in the escape of a Kentucky slave.*

taking with him several slaves, including some who belonged to his uncle. They traveled at night. During the day, while the slaves hid in the woods, Fairfield went out to buy food and other supplies. They succeeded in reaching Canada safely, and Fairfield decided to make Canada his home.

But he was soon back at work helping other slaves escape. In fact, it became his regular business. Many slaves paid him, and he accepted their money, although if they had none he helped them just the same. Some fugitives hired him to go south to rescue the husbands, wives, or children they had left behind. That became a specialty for him.

Fairfield made trips south to Alabama, Louisiana, Mississippi, and Tennessee, as well as Kentucky. He posed variously as a slaveholder, a Negro trader,

An early illustration depicting runaways fleeing in a rainstorm along the freedom trail north.

and a peddler of eggs and chickens. He would announce that he was a Virginian and express strong pro-slavery feelings. In that way, he gained the confidence of slaveholders. Meanwhile, he secretly let it be known to their slaves that he was there to help them. Then he would suddenly disappear, and so would several local slaves.

During the twelve years Fairfield engaged in his special business, he managed to rescue several hundred slaves, including one party of twenty-eight. He was shot once, arrested several times, and imprisoned more than once. But he did not stop. He died in 1860, and was believed to have been killed in a slave revolt in Tennessee.

Laura Haviland was a Quaker woman in Michigan who in 1837 started a school called the Raisen Institute. It was based on the concept, revolutionary for the time, of mixed education — both as to race and sex. She operated an Underground Railroad station and several times accompanied fugitive slaves all the way to Canada.

In 1847, a fugitive named John White, who worked on a farm near the Raisen Institute, asked her for help in rescuing his wife, Jane, from slavery in Kentucky. Haviland agreed, and traveled to the Stevens plantation, where Jane White was a slave. With the help of a free mulatto woman, Haviland posed as "Aunt Smith" from Georgia and managed to let Jane White know that plans were in the making to rescue her. Then she returned to Michigan.

Laura Haviland, noted abolitionist of Adrian, Michigan, displays slave restraining devices, including an iron collar, knee stiffener, and handcuffs, collected while traveling to Louisiana.

Soon John White could not wait any longer. He went to Kentucky himself and conducted his wife and a friend to Indiana. But a slave hunter caught up with them. John White managed to escape, but he became separated from his wife. Later, he learned that she was dead.

Dr. Alexander Milton Ross was a Canadian ornithologist who traveled into the Deep South under the guise of collecting bird specimens. Although he did not personally conduct slaves to freedom, he gave them the hope that they could escape and directions for where to go. He later wrote of his trip to Mississippi:

I made frequent visits to the surrounding plantations seizing every favourable opportunity to converse with the more intelligent of the slaves. Many of these negroes had heard of Canada from the negroes brought from Virginia and the border Slave States; but the impression they had was, that Canada, being so far away, it would be useless to try and reach it. On these excursions I was usually accompanied by one or two smart, intelligent slaves, to whom I felt I could trust the secret of my visit. In this way, I succeeded in circulating a knowledge of Canada, and the best means of reaching that country, to all the plantations for many miles around Vicksburg . . .

Later, in Columbus, Mississippi, Ross befriended a slave he called Joe, who wanted to run away to Canada. Ross gave Joe directions, a compass, a pistol, and a knife. When Joe was discovered missing, Ross was arrested on suspicion of helping him. In the midst of Ross's trial, Joe appeared in the courtroom, to the astonishment of everyone. He begged his master for forgiveness and said he had only meant to travel to a neighboring plantation to visit his sick brother, but had fallen and broken his ankle and had not been able to move for two days.

The master was dumbfounded by Joe's appearance, and Ross took the opportunity to claim a favor of

Dr. Alexander M. Ross traveled throughout the South where he advised many slaves on the best escape routes to Canada.

him — not to punish Joe. The master said he would not.

Two years later, Ross was eating in a restaurant in Boston when a black waiter approached him and identified himself as Joe. Within days after Ross's trial, Joe and his brother had run away, following the directions Ross had provided and had reached Canada, where Joe's brother still lived.

Many former fugitives later became conductors. William Wells Brown escaped from St. Louis and settled at first in Cleveland, Ohio. There he worked on lake steamers, which plied the waters of the Great Lakes between the United States port cities and those in Canada. He later wrote that between May 1 and December 1, 1842, he carried sixty-nine runaways to Canada.

Most black conductors worked in the free states, for it was too dangerous to go into the South. Many southern states had laws excluding free blacks from within their borders. Travel for free blacks was severely restricted, and free blacks had so few rights that they were in constant danger of being sold into slavery even if they had papers to prove they were not slaves.

Some fugitives took the risk and became conductors in the South when they went back to rescue family members, but did not continue to do so once they had either succeeded or failed in that personal mission. But one woman continued even after her own family members were safely in freedom. The most famous conductor on the Underground Railroad, Harriet Tubman, rescued several brothers and sisters as well as her parents, along with hundreds of other slaves.

6
Harriet Tubman, the Woman Called Moses

The most famous conductor on the Underground Railroad was an escaped slave herself. Harriet Tubman was born on the Edward Brodas plantation in Dorchester County, Maryland, in 1820 or 1821. One of several children (perhaps as many as eleven) born to Harriet Green, who was usually called Old Rit, and Benjamin Ross, Harriet was called Araminta when she was a baby. Later, she was called Harriet, after her mother.

When she was little, Harriet was cared for by an old woman slave whose job it was to look after the small children while their parents worked in the fields. But when Harriet turned six, she was old enough to work. Her master hired her out to local people who worked her hard and treated her cruelly.

But she was back on the Brodas plantation when she received a severe head wound that would affect her for the rest of her life, causing her to lose consciousness at any time and without warning. Her injury occurred when a slave was trying to escape. Harriet attempted to block the way of the overseer who was after him. The brick the overseer threw was intended for the runaway, but it hit Harriet.

In 1848, Harriet married John Tubman, a free black whose parents had been set free by their master on the master's death. Although she was happy with John, Harriet could not help worrying, for as a slave she could be sold away from her husband at any time. She talked about escaping to the North, but John told her such talk was foolish. When she persisted, he threatened to tell the master. Harriet was shocked. The hurt she felt was greater than any physical pain she had ever suffered. And from that time on, she was afraid of her husband.

In 1849 the young heir to the Brodas estate died, and the estate was broken up. Among the first slaves to be sold were two of Harriet's sisters. Tubman knew she would soon suffer the same fate and was determined to run away. But she was afraid she might fall into one of her strange, unpredictable sleeps and be caught. So, she persuaded three of her brothers to go with her. They set off one night, but the brothers became fearful and forced Harriet to return to the plantation with them.

Two days later, Harriet Tubman learned that she

Known as the Moses of her people, Harriet Tubman, an escaped slave from Maryland, became the most famous conductor on the Underground Railroad.

and her brothers had been sold to a Georgia slave
trader and that they were to be sent south with a
chain gang. She was determined not to be sold south,
never to see her family again. She later explained,
"I had reasoned this out in my mind; there was one
of two things I had a *right* to, liberty or death; if I
could not have one, I would have the other; for no
man should take me alive; I should fight for my
liberty as long as my strength lasted . . ."

That evening, when the work day was over, Tubman returned to the quarter singing the words of a
spiritual that began, "When that old chariot comes,
I'm going to leave you." It was her way of telling
the other slaves what she planned to do. In the cabin
she shared with her husband, she waited until he fell
asleep, then quietly prepared to go. She took the ash
cake she had made for their breakfast the next day
and put it and a piece of salt herring into a bandana.
Then, with one last look at her husband, she was
gone.

As soon as she was off the plantation, Tubman
headed for nearby Bucktown and a farmhouse where
a white woman lived. Earlier that same year, 1849,
the woman had driven past the Brodas plantation
fields in a wagon and stopped to talk to Harriet. She
asked how Harriet had gotten the scar on her forehead, and Tubman told her. The woman said she
lived on a farm near Bucktown. After that, whenever
she saw Harriet in the fields, she stopped to talk with

her. One day, she said quietly, "Harriet, if you ever need any help, let me know."

Tubman was not sure she could trust this white woman, but she had no other choice. She did need help. When the woman answered Harriet Tubman's soft knock on the door, she did not seem surprised to see her. She gave Harriet the names of two places where it would be safe for her to stop.

Tubman made her way through the woods to the first place, frightened at every sound, imagining the newspaper ads and handbills that would soon be issued, describing the way she looked and offering a reward for her capture. She reached the house the following morning. The woman fed her, then handed her a broom and told her to sweep the yard. Tubman realized that would make her look as if she belonged there. That night the woman's husband loaded a wagon with produce and told Harriet to climb in. Then he threw some blankets over her. Although Tubman knew the man might be taking her back to the Brodas plantation, she was so tired that she fell asleep.

Some hours later the wagon stopped. Harriet was instantly awake. The man told her to follow the river to the next place, to travel only at night, and to keep off the roads, lest she be found by the patrols that were out hunting for her. Tubman followed the river. By the time she reached Pennsylvania she had traveled ninety miles from the Brodas plantation.

She had been rowed for miles up the Choptank River by a white man, had been hidden in the attic of a Quaker farm, had been hidden in a haystack on a farm belonging to German immigrants, and had spent a week hiding in a potato hole in a cabin belonging to a family of free blacks. She had spent nights in the woods and had quieted the growling in her stomach with berries. But she had reached free territory.

She later said that when she reached Pennsylvania, "I looked at my hands to see if I was the same person. There was such a glory over everything. The sun came up like gold through the trees, and I felt like I was in heaven."

Harriet spent two years in Philadelphia, where she

William Still became an active conductor on the Underground Railroad in Philadelphia where he later settled and wrote one of the early and most extensive accounts of the Underground Railroad.

found work as a cook in a hotel. She met William Still of the Philadelphia Vigilance Committee, which had been founded by a group of blacks and a few whites to help fugitive slaves and keep them from falling into the hands of slave hunters. Harriet Tubman was fascinated by Still's tales of other escaped slaves who had made their way to Philadelphia. Soon she was visiting the offices of the Vigilance Committee nearly every night after work. She learned about the extensive Underground Railroad network in that area of the country. She met individuals and groups of escaped slaves and heard their stories firsthand.

From time to time she heard news of her parents and sisters and brothers. One night she learned that her sister Mary and her children were about to be sold. Mary's husband, a free black named John Bowley, had asked his friends in the Underground Railroad to help the family escape. A Quaker friend of Bowley's had helped him make plans to get the family to Baltimore, but someone was needed to get them from Baltimore to Philadelphia. Harriet volunteered, and refused to listen to William Still's warnings that it was too dangerous for her, a fugitive herself, to bring out a family of escaped slaves. All she knew was that her sister and her children were about to be sold. She could not let that happen.

By the time all the necessary arrangements had been made, Mary Bowley and her two children, one a baby, had already been taken to a slave pen outside the courthouse in Cambridge, Maryland, to be put up at auction. Fortunately, during the first round of the auction, no one had bid on them. During the lunch recess, John Bowley entered the courthouse and presented a piece of paper to the guard at the slave pen. The message was supposed to be from "his master, the auctioneer," and it instructed the guard to let John take the woman, Mary, and her children over to the inn where the auctioneer was having lunch. Bowley told the guard that the auctioneer thought he had a buyer for the family. The guard opened the door of the slave pen and herded the little group out.

Once on the street, John Bowley and his family walked quickly to the home of his Quaker friend,

The plight of the runaway is captured in this classic painting "The Ride for Liberty-The Fugitive Slaves" by the American painter Eastman Johnson.

where they hid in the attic until dark. Then they were taken to the kitchen for supper, after which they were transported by wagon to the river. They were rowed out to a fishing boat, which John then sailed up the Chesapeake Bay to Baltimore. As the fishing boat reached Baltimore, Bowley looked for and found a yellow light and a blue light, close together. He put his family in the dinghy and rowed toward the lights, which turned out to be barn lanterns with colored shades. At the barn, the family were loaded into a wagon filled with potatoes and onions and driven to a stable, where they stayed all day. That night, after being fed, they climbed into another wagon and rode a short distance to the back door of a brick house. A short, stocky black woman was waiting for them in the kitchen. It was Harriet.

After spending a week with her sister and family at the brick house in Baltimore, Tubman guided her small party from station to station until they reached Philadelphia. Her success gave her the courage to return to Dorchester County, Maryland, to bring out more members of her family, and in the spring of 1851 she conducted one of her brothers and two other men to safety.

That summer she worked in a Cape May, New Jersey, hotel to save enough money for another trip back to Maryland, this time to persuade her husband to return to the North with her. She had not seen John Tubman in two years, and during that time her fear and distrust had faded, giving way to her sweet memories of their time together. In the fall of 1851, dressed in a man's suit and hat, she made her way to the old Brodas plantation and to the cabin in the slave quarter that she had shared with John. She found him there, with a young new wife named Caroline. When Harriet told John why she had come, he laughed mockingly at her. That laugh would ring in her ears for years to come. Remembering that John had once threatened to tell the master that she was planning to escape, Harriet realized it was dangerous for her to stay around long. She moved quietly through the quarter, rapping softly on doors. By midnight she had collected a small group of slaves who wanted to be free, and had started back to Philadelphia with them.

By the time she returned to Philadelphia, stories of the harsh effects of the new fugitive slave law were rife. Runaways were being caught and arrested in such formerly safe cities as Boston, where a young fugitive named Thomas Sims became the first slave to be sent back into slavery by Massachusetts since the Revolution. Transported to Savannah, Georgia, by a ship chartered by the United States government, he was publicly whipped and then imprisoned for two months, after which he was sold and resold. (Years later, the story of Thomas Sims took a happy turn, for after the outbreak of the Civil War he managed to escape to the Union forces near Vicksburg, Virginia, where he was welcomed as a hero and sent back North, never to be a slave again.)

At the age of 23, Thomas Sims became the first runaway sent back into slavery by Massachusetts since the Revolution.

But these stories did not dissuade Harriet Tubman from returning south to rescue more slaves. They simply made her realize that from now on she could not just take them to Philadelphia and be assured of their safety; she would have to guide them all the way to Canada. And what made her decision even more remarkable was that she was now determined to rescue not just members of her own family but any slave who had the courage to go with her.

By the time she returned to the South in December 1851, Harriet Tubman was the subject of legend among southern slaves, to whom she was known as Moses. On this trip, she brought out eleven slaves, including one of her brothers and his wife.

It was a large group for the Underground Railroad,

and at least one "stationmaster" refused to help them, saying they were too many and it wasn't safe, since his place had been searched just the week before. Tubman had to use all her powers of positive thinking and storytelling abilities to keep up the spirits of her charges until she could get them to the next station.

In Wilmington, Delaware, they were welcomed by the Quaker stationmaster Thomas Garrett, who concealed them in a secret room behind a wall of shoe boxes. He gave them all new shoes, for it was winter and they would need something on their feet if they were to travel farther north. He also provided carriages to take them to their next destination. Reaching Philadelphia, they stopped only long enough to check in with William Still at the Vigilance Committee, who quickly recorded their names and gave them money for their trip to Burlington, New Jersey. From there they went to New York City, and from there to Syracuse in upstate New York. In Syracuse, Tubman met the Reverend J. W. Loguen, the unofficial "King of the Underground Railroad." He sent them to the next stop, Rochester, New York, where they probably stayed with Frederick Douglass, who later wrote of the time he harbored eleven fugitives and had some difficulty providing so many with food and shelter.

Finally, in late December 1851, almost a month from the start of their journey, Harriet Tubman and her band arrived in St. Catharines, a town in what

Many African American runaways, including these settlers of Windsor, Ontario, built thriving communities in Canada.

is now Ontario, Canada. She spent the winter there with them, for she could not just leave them to fend for themselves. She and they worked to pay for the rent on a small house to live in and for food to eat. Harriet had spent several years being able to quit one job and look for another, but the experience was new and marvelous for the former slaves. There were things about Canada that Tubman, too, found marvelous. Black men could vote, hold office, sit on juries, and live in any part of town they chose. St. Catharines had many ex-slaves as residents. Many had prospered. Tubman decided that St. Catharines was where she wanted to make her own home. But for many years it would serve less as a home than as a home base, for Harriet intended to keep on returning to the South on her missions of rescue.

For the next six years, from 1852 to 1857, the woman called Moses returned again and again to Maryland to bring out slaves. Her life developed an unchanging pattern. She would make two trips south a year, one in the spring and one in the fall. She would spend the winter in St. Catharines and the summer in Cape May, New Jersey, or elsewhere, working in hotels to raise money for her trips.

Although southern slaveholders and law enforcement authorities offered a twelve-thousand-dollar reward for her capture, she was never turned in. Partly this was because she made sure she would not be informed on. She always carried a gun, and if any slave with whom she was traveling asked to go back, she threatened to use it, explaining that she could not trust him or her not to tell.

She always announced her presence at a plantation by singing a meaningful spiritual. She carried paregoric, a tranquilizer, to quiet crying babies. She seemed to have a sixth sense about when danger was near and had an uncanny ability to make the right decisions about avoiding that danger. She persuaded groups of slaves to wade across rivers, to spend nights in the woods huddling together for warmth, to overcome fears that might have paralyzed them. Most of the people she helped were strangers to her, although she did rescue several brothers and sisters.

From time to time she had thought about rescuing her parents, but she could not come up with a good plan. All the people she had conducted to freedom

A photo of Harriet Tubman in mid-life.

had been young and strong. She knew her parents would not survive a journey through woods and swamps, in the rain and cold. She had to put such ideas aside.

Then, in June 1857, she began to have dreams that her parents were about to be sold. She trusted her dreams as premonitions and decided that she must rescue her parents immediately. She traveled by train to Dorchester County, judging rightly that no one would suspect that a fugitive slave would take the risk of publicly going back into slave territory. Arriving in Bucktown, she put on a large sunbonnet and bought a pair of chickens from a free black family. Walking with the bent posture of an old, old woman who must have come from the market, she made her way to the old Brodas plantation. She waited until dark, then approached her parents' cabin. They were overjoyed to see her and willing to take the risk of going north with her.

Tubman sneaked over to the next plantation and stole the only available horse, an old nag. She then stole an old wagon from Dr. Thompson, made her parents as comfortable as possible in it, and set off. They traveled at night, spending the days in the woods off the road. Three nights later, they reached the home of Thomas Garrett in Wilmington, and from there followed Tubman's usual route to Philadelphia and New York, to Syracuse and Rochester, and finally to St. Catharines. It was one of the easiest trips she had ever made.

When her days of traveling drew to a close Harriet Tubman purchased this house in Auburn, New York.

St. Catharines was cold in June 1857, and Harriet realized her parents would not be comfortable there. So she bought a small house for them in Auburn, New York, southwest of Syracuse. It was not as safe as Canada, but it was warmer. The Reverend J. W. Loguen in Syracuse could look in on them from time to time when she was gone.

That fall she returned to Maryland. Over the next several weeks, sixty Dorchester County slaves arrived at the headquarters of the Vigilance Committee. Tubman had not led all of them to Philadelphia, but she had given them directions as to how to get there on their own. She spent the winter in St. Catharines, doing odd jobs and trying to earn enough money to pay the mortgage on her parents' home in Auburn.

In April the Reverend Loguen brought a white man to see her. His name was John Brown, and he had a plan to free a large number of slaves. He would establish a stronghold in the mountains of Virginia and send out a call to all nearby slaves to join him. He wanted Tubman to tell him how to get the slaves to Canada. He also wanted her to help him raise a small army in Canada to assist him in carrying out his plan. Harriet agreed to help him.

By the fall of 1858 Harriet Tubman had helped over three hundred slaves to reach the North and freedom. According to a report in *The National Anti-Slavery Standard*, published in New York, on a convention of slaveholders in Cambridge, Maryland, in November 1858, "The operation of the Underground Railroad on the Maryland border, within the last few years has been so extensive that in some neighborhoods the whole slave population have made their escape, and the Convention is a result of the general panic on the part of the owners of this specie of property . . ."

In the fall of 1858 Tubman traveled to Boston to make her first speech before an anti-slavery society meeting. Her recollections of some of her trips south inspired and awed her audience, and thereafter she was in considerable demand as a speaker at such meetings. Many people suggested that she devote herself to the anti-slavery lecture circuit and not return to Maryland, and for a while she spent most of her time lecturing, traveling on trains without fearing capture, and being treated with great respect and admiration.

During that fall and winter in Boston, Tubman met with John Brown several times. She told him all she knew about the routes she had used to the North and the hiding places along the way, even drawing rough maps for him. She had suggested at their first meeting that he put his plan into action on July 4, the anniversary of American independence, and as spring arrived and turned into summer, she expected to hear from him again.

But while John Brown wrote often of her in letters to friends and associates, he did not contact her. Or, if he did, she did not respond. She may have been influenced by Frederick Douglass or others who re-

Affectionately Yours

John. Brown

John Brown, best remembered for the Harpers Ferry raid, met and often wrote about Harriet Tubman in his correspondence to friends.

fused to have anything to do with Brown's plot, saying it was too dangerous.

July 4 came and went and nothing happened. Then in the fall of 1859 an event that would shape the course of United States history occurred. On October 16–17, John Brown, leading twenty-two men, seventeen of whom were white, attacked the United States arsenal at Harpers Ferry, Virginia. Federal troops commanded by Colonel Robert E. Lee put down the assault, killing ten men, including two of Brown's sons. Brown himself was captured and later hanged. Before he died, he made an eloquent speech, saying in part, "I believe that to have interfered as I have done, as I have always freely admitted I have done, in behalf of [God's] despised poor, I did no wrong but right."

John Brown was regarded as a villain by slaveholders, who, fearing a slave uprising in response to Brown's hanging, cracked down on their slaves even more than usual. But Brown was considered a martyr by those who opposed slavery, including Harriet Tubman. She wished he had done more planning. He had not spread the word to local slaves to help him or even let them know why he was planning the raid. If he had made his objectives more widely known, he might have had some help. Tubman resolved to do something to honor his memory, although she did not know what.

By 1860 Tubman had grown tired of the anti-slavery lecture circuit and wanted to return to Mary-

land, where by 1860 the reward offered for her capture was forty thousand dollars. She earned enough
money to finance a trip and headed south in late
November.

In December she brought out a party of six, including three children, aged six, four, and three
months, and saw them safely to Philadelphia. It
would be her last trip as a conductor on the Underground Railroad. The North and the South were
soon at war, and with President Abraham Lincoln's
Emancipation Proclamation ending slavery in the
Confederate States her Underground Railroad work
was over.

7
Railroad Songs

Often, the first people to help a fugitive slave were fellow slaves. On large southern plantations, the slave quarters were usually quite far away from the main house. A runaway could sometimes make his way to the "quarter" of a plantation, where courageous slaves would hide and feed him, even though they risked a terrible beating or being sold if they were caught.

In spite of the distance between plantations, over the years slaves on different plantations had developed many ways of communicating with one another, and the "plantation grapevine" was very effective.

Music and song were important for the slaves, and not just for making their workday go faster or for keeping up their spirits. In the early days of slavery, slaves used drums to communicate with one another across long distances, just as they had in Africa. When it finally became clear to slave masters that drums were being used to send messages from plantation to plantation, they outlawed drums. But that did not stop the slaves. Instead, they used their feet. They were still allowed to have dances, and they devised a clever way to make sounds with their bare feet on wooden floors that approximated drum sounds so closely that only the keenest ears could tell the difference.

Slaves found other ways to communicate with one another. Most converted to Christianity at the urging or on the orders of their masters. They took

This painting, "The Old Plantation," captures the many West African musical influences among Charleston slaves.

the idea of Christian hymns and developed their own songs, called spirituals. Also called sorrow songs, they expressed the suffering of the slaves and their longing for the peaceful kingdom of heaven. The slaves took especially to heart the Bible stories about the Israelites in slavery in Egypt and of their flight to freedom. Many spirituals are about Israelites.

It was dangerous to talk about freedom and running away, so these songs were a safe way to express what the slaves could not say openly. The words of spirituals could also have double meanings and be used to send secret messages from one person to another.

Harriet Tubman, the woman called Moses because she conducted so many of her people to freedom, got her nickname from the words of the song "Go Down Moses":

When Israel was in Egypt's Land,
Let my people go.
Oppressed so hard they could not stand,
Let my people go.
Go down, Moses, way down in Egypt's Land,
Tell old Pharaoh, let my people go . . .
No more shall they in bondage toil,
Let my people go.
Let them come out with Egypt's spoil,
Let my people go.

Egypt's land was the South; Pharaoh was the slave-holder.

When Tubman, who was herself born a slave, decided to escape, she sang a spiritual to announce to the other slaves her intention to go:

> When that old chariot comes,
> I'm going to leave you,
> I'm bound for the promised land,
> Friends, I'm going to leave you.
>
> I'm sorry, friends, to leave you,
> Farewell! Oh, farewell!
> But I'll meet you in the morning,
> Farewell! Oh, farewell!
>
> I'll meet you in the morning,
> When I reach the promised land;
> On the other side of Jordan,
> For I'm bound for the promised land.

The River Jordan, located in present-day northern Israel, was the scene of the baptism of Jesus. In spirituals, it is the river that must be crossed before one reaches the promised land (often the free states or Canada).

The song "Steal Away to Jesus" could also have a double meaning and was sung as an invitation to slaves to run away:

Steal away, steal away to Jesus,
Steal away, steal away home.
I ain't got long to stay here.
My Lord calls me, he calls me by thunder,
The trumpet sounds within my soul.
I ain't got long to stay here.

The song "Wade in the Water" could be sung to warn an escaped slave that the master and his bloodhounds were on the trail. The only way to throw a bloodhound off a human scent was to get into the water. Slaves would sing, "Wade in the water, wade in the water. Children, God going to trouble the water," and that would send a message of warning to the runaway.

The spiritual "Get On Board, Little Children," sometimes also called "The Gospel Train," referred directly to the Underground Railroad:

Get on board, little children,
Get on board, little children,
Get on board, little children,
There's room for many more.

The gospel train is coming,
I hear it just at hand.
I hear the car wheels moving
And rumbling through the land.

Underground Railroad lore includes the story of a

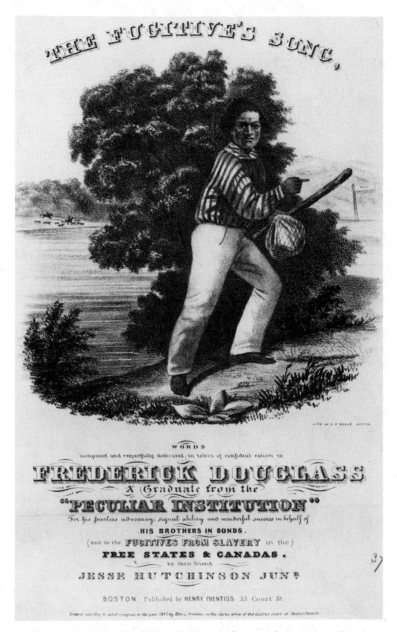

The escape of Frederick Douglass inspired a song by composer Jesse Hutchinson.

one-legged sailor named Peg Leg Joe, a free black man. There is no way to know if he really existed or if he is just a myth. But the story is that he would hire himself out to plantation owners as a handyman. Then he would make friends with the slaves and teach them what appeared to be a harmless folk song.

But hidden in the words of the song were directions for following the Underground Railroad. The song was called "Follow the Drinking Gourd," which was a nickname for the Big Dipper, which points to the North Star. These were the lyrics:

Follow the drinking gourd! Follow the drinking
    gourd.
For the old man is a-waiting for to carry you to
    freedom
If you follow the drinking gourd.
When the sun comes back, and the first quail
    calls,
Follow the drinking gourd.
For the old man is a-waiting for to carry you to
    freedom
If you follow the drinking gourd.

The riverbank makes a very good road,
The dead trees will show you the way.
Left foot, peg foot, traveling on,
Follow the drinking gourd.

The river ends between two hills,
Follow the drinking gourd.
There's another river on the other side,
Follow the drinking gourd.

When the great big river meets the little river,
Follow the drinking gourd.
For the old man is a-waiting for to carry you to
    freedom
If you follow the drinking gourd.

"When the sun comes back" meant that the slaves should travel in the springtime. The river that "ends between two hills" was the Tombigbee River in Mississippi. The second was the Tennessee River, and the "great big river" was the Ohio River.

After teaching the slaves the song, Peg Leg Joe would leave the plantation, promising to meet them at the "great big river." When they arrived, he would ferry them across to the free states on the other side, where they transferred onto one of the Underground Railroad lines to Canada.

8
The Train Robbers

The Underground Railroad had "passengers" and "cargo." It had "depots" and "station-masters" and "conductors." All these terms were used to describe the people and places on the Underground Railroad. One term that was never used was "train robbers," and yet that's what the slave catchers were to the Underground Railroad. They did their best to derail the trains and rob them of their human cargo.

Professional slave hunters caught slaves for a living. Like bounty hunters, who went after criminals and collected rewards for their capture "dead or alive," they aimed to collect the rewards offered by slaveholders for the return of their human property.

Slave masters placed advertisements in newspapers

describing their runaways and offering rewards for their capture. Such notices filled southern and northern newspapers, town bulletin boards, and even covered roadside trees. Most people who saw or read the notices either determined to be on the lookout for runaways or to ignore them as none of their business. But for professional slave hunters, answering the advertisements was their business.

Here is a typical advertisement:

LOST
Four Dollars Reward

RAN AWAY from the Subscriber, living in Abbet's-Town, York County, on the 8th of May last, a SERVANT BOY, named DAVID BURNSIDES, a Country-born, about 4 Feet 6 or 7 Inches high, supposed to be about 20 Years of Age, short fair Hair, has a remarkably large Mouth, a small Scar near one of his Eyes, very small Feet, and is of a fair Complexion: Had on, and took with him, an old Felt Hat, a dirty yellow Hunting-Shirt, brown Cloth Overalls, and Two Tow shirts; he was at Mr. Leamon's, his former Master, on the 17th or 18th of May last, whom he informed that he was a Freeman, and, after remaining there Two or Three Days, he stole a Plush Vest and other Clothing: He says his Father lives near the Blue-Ball-Tavern. Whoever secures the said Servant, so that his

$100 REWARD!

RANAWAY

From the undersigned, living on Current River, about twelve miles above Doniphan, in Ripley County, Mo., on 2nd of March, 1860, **A NE GRO MAN,** about 30 years old, weighs about 160 pounds; high forehead, with a scar on it; had on brown pants and coat very much worn, and an old black wool hat; shoes size No. 11.

The above reward will be given to any person who may apprehend this said negro out of the State; and fifty dollars if apprehended in this State outside of Ripley county, or $25 if taken in Ripley county.

APOS TUCKER.

This ad for a runaway slave is typical of the many handbills and posters that were found in many American communities.

Master may get him again, shall receive the above Reward, and reasonable Charges.

WILLIAM MACKEY

July 8, 1790

Professional slave catchers either bred, or bought from breeders, special bloodhounds that were often called "Negro dogs" and that were trained to trail fugitives by picking up a human scent and following it for miles. In 1849 a Mississippi slave master praised the talents of a slave catcher he had hired: "He follows a negro with his dogs 36 hours after he has passed and never fails to overtake him. It is his profession and he makes some $600 per annum at it."

The dogs could be vicious. Usually their job was only to find the fugitive, not maul him. But if a slave owner allowed it, the dogs would be set upon the poor slave. One Louisiana planter's dogs "treed" a runaway and then pulled him down from the tree, biting him ferociously.

There were ways for fugitives to outsmart the dogs. One was to take to the water, because the dogs could not find a human scent in water. An Underground Railroad stationmaster in Denmark, Iowa, Deacon Theron Trowbridge of the Denmark Congregationalist Church, was said to have invented another way. He put strychnine, a deadly poison, in corn sticks and set them out for the dogs. They died soon after eating them. He called these poison-laced corn sticks "hush puppies."

Professional slave catchers lived and worked in both the South and the North. One of the most enterprising in the North was F. H. Pettis, a lawyer in New York City. He advertised his services in southern newspapers. His advertisement in the June 9, 1840, issue of the Charleston, South Carolina, Courier, claimed that he had much experience in "causing fugitive slaves to be secured." All a slave master had to do was send him a description of the runaway, power of attorney [legal permission to act on behalf of the master], and a fee of twenty dollars. "When the slave shall have been secured and handed over to the master, $100 additional charge will be made."

Professional slave hunters were not always concerned with whether they caught the right person.
Many did not bother to go through the legal for-
malities of taking the slave before a court, but instead
took the fugitive back to the South as quickly as
possible. There were several famous cases of free
blacks living in the North being kidnapped by slave
catchers and enslaved. The federal law of 1793 was
on the side of the slave catchers. It provided that
only a federal judge or state magistrate could decide
the status of alleged fugitive slaves, thereby denying
them the right to testify on their own behalf or the
right to trial by jury.

But local sentiment in the North was often against
the slave hunters, especially when they were clearly
guilty of kidnapping. This sentiment was evident in
Philadelphia in the early years of the United States.
One of the escaped slaves Philadelphia Quakers
helped was Richard Allen, who went on to become
a minister and to found the African Methodist Epis-
copal Church. After twenty years of living in freedom, he was arrested by a slave catcher as a fugitive.
The slave catcher went through legal channels and
there was a trial. But the case against Allen was
dismissed after he proved he had been living as a
free man for more than twenty years.

Allen then turned around and had the slave
catcher arrested for kidnapping. The slave catcher
spent three months in jail because he was unable to
post a bond of eight hundred dollars. There is no

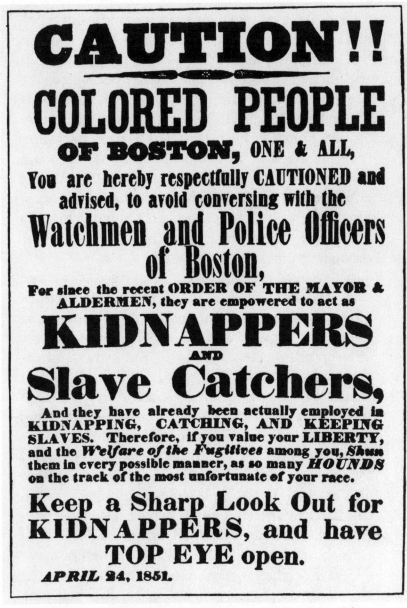

An abolitionist poster of Boston, 1851, warning of the results of the Fugitive Slave Law.

telling how long he might have spent in jail if Allen had not decided to drop the charges.

The organization of vigilance committees in Philadelphia and other northern cities grew out of the need to resist the actions of the slave catchers. Arising in the middle 1830s, these committees were formed primarily by blacks, although some whites were involved in the organizations. They raised money, mostly from local black communities, to feed and clothe and shelter runaways. They also worked hard to prevent the runaways from being kidnapped and taken back to the South, and that was where the need for vigilance came in.

There were many slave agents in these cities, and some posed as friends of the slaves in order to learn more about the underground network that helped them. The New York Vigilance Committee made a "Slaveholders Directory" listing the names and addresses of lawyers, police, and others who "lend themselves to kidnapping." Some whites helped support the work of the vigilance committees and warned them of dangerous people.

William Still first served as the corresponding secretary on the Philadelphia Vigilance Committee and later headed it. He kept detailed records of the escaped slaves the committee helped, and later published the first history of the Underground Railroad, titled *Underground Railroad Records*, in 1872.

Some northern states passed laws aimed at the slave hunters. Some of these laws gave slaves the

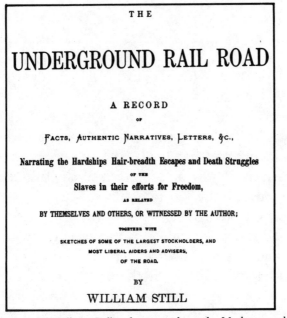

The title page of William Still's classic work on the Underground Railroad.

right to testify on their own behalf and the right to a jury trial. Other states had laws that imposed criminal penalties for kidnapping.

Pennsylvania passed an anti-kidnapping law in 1826. Under that law, in 1837 a slave hunter named Edward Prigg was found guilty of kidnapping after he seized a slave woman named Mary Morgan and her children and returned them to their Maryland owner. Prigg had not bothered to get a warrant for Mary Morgan's arrest.

Prigg's attorneys appealed his conviction to the United States Supreme Court, arguing that he was within his rights under the Fugitive Slave Act of 1793. The Supreme Court handed down its decision in *Prigg v. Pennsylvania* (the v. means versus, or against) in 1842. The Court upheld the slave law of 1793 and ruled that a slaveholder's right to his property overrode any state legislation to the contrary. At the same time, the Court held that enforcement of the fugitive slave clause of the Constitution was a federal responsibility and that states need not cooperate in any way.

Many northern states saw the last part of the Court's ruling as a go-ahead to pass a new series of personal liberty laws that barred the use of state authorities or property in the recapture of fugitives. Nine such laws were passed between 1842 and 1850.

Infuriated southerners then pressed for a new federal fugitive slave law, and won what they considered a great victory with the passage of the Fugituve Slave Law of 1850. The law denied captured blacks any legal power to prove their freedom. It required United States marshalls and deputies to help slave owners capture their property and fined them $1000 if they refused.

In some ways, the law did just what southern slave masters hoped it would. In the decade of the 1850s, 322 fugitive slaves caught in the North were returned to their masters, and only eleven were declared free. But the law only served to make abolitionists more determined to help fugitives. That same decade of the 1850s also saw the greatest activity on the Underground Railroad.

9
The Passengers

The Underground Railroad story that has come down through history understates the role of the escaped slaves themselves. They tend to be portrayed as passive victims who would never have succeeded without help. Although it is true that most depended on the help of others, any slave who got very far in his or her attempt to escape had to be strong, courageous, and clever.

This was especially true in the days before the Underground Railroad became well-organized. Josiah Henson managed to reach Canada largely on his own.

Born in Charles County, Maryland, on June 15, 1789, he was owned by three different masters before he made his escape from slavery. One master beat

Josiah Henson, a runaway, whose story inspired Harriet Beecher Stowe to write Uncle Tom's Cabin.

Henson with a stake, breaking his arm and perhaps both his shoulder blades and maiming him for life.

Henson believed that his third master was a fair man, on the whole, and he worked hard to please him. He was so loyal and hardworking that his master even trusted him to take eighteen other slaves to Kentucky. Still trusted by his master, Henson remained in Kentucky three years, became a preacher, and earned money with which he hoped to purchase his freedom. His owner agreed to sell him for $450. Henson paid him $350 and signed a note promising to pay the rest as soon as he could. But then his owner said the price was $1000, and there was nothing Henson could do about it. It was his word against his master's. But still Henson did not run away.

Henson learned by the plantation grapevine that he was going to be sold, and at first he could not believe it. Then his master informed him that he was to accompany the master's nephew to New Orleans. Henson realized that he was being tricked, and that once they reached New Orleans he would be put up at auction at the active slave market there. He felt betrayed by his master and was furious. One night on the way to New Orleans, he picked up an axe and was about to kill the nephew, but he realized that his Christian faith would not allow him to do it. He continued on to New Orleans, knowing that he would be sold and that he would probably never see his wife and children again.

Fortunately, the nephew fell ill and asked Henson

A relic of the era of slavery is captured in this photo of an auction house advertising "Negro Sales."

to take him back home to Kentucky. Once Henson reached his owner's plantation and was reunited with his wife and family, there was no question in his mind that they would run away to Canada.

After making careful plans, Henson and his family started out. He carried his two smallest children in a knapsack on his back. His wife and their two older children walked. Keeping to the cover of the woods and traveling only at night, they reached the Ohio River, crossed over into Indiana, and two weeks later reached Cincinnati. Near Cincinnati, a tribe of Indians helped them reach Sandusky, and there a Scottish steamer captain transported them to Buffalo, New York. On October 28, 1830, about six weeks after they had crossed the Ohio River, the Henson family reached Canada.

The Josiah Henson House is a local historic site better known as Uncle Tom's Cabin in Dresden, Ontario.

Their first house in Canada was an old shack.
Henson had to shoo several pigs out of it before they
could move in. But he soon found a job and was able
to find better quarters for his family. Once he had
his own family settled, Henson turned his attention
to helping other newly arrived fugitives. At first he
assisted them informally. Several years later, in 1842
he helped found the Dawn Institute, where fugitive
slaves were taught trades so they could support themselves and their families in Canada.

One fugitive whom Henson might have aided
when he himself was newly arrived in Canada was
Eliza Harris, born a slave in Kentucky a few miles
from the Ohio River. She had just one child, having
lost two other children when they were infants, and
this child, a daughter, was the most important thing
in her life.

Her master and mistress treated her well, but when
they needed money they decided to sell Eliza's child.
Eliza could not bear to lose her two-year-old daughter
and decided to flee. It was winter, but that same
night she set out, carrying the sleeping little girl,
and made her way to the Ohio River. She thought
it would be frozen over and she could walk across.
But when she reached it, she found that the ice had
broken up and big chunks were floating in the open
water.

Eliza went to a house nearby, where she was taken
in and allowed to spend the night and the following
day. But by the next evening slave hunters were in

the area looking for her, and she knew she had to risk the river crossing. When the slave hunters rode up to the house on horseback, Eliza ran out the back, carrying her little girl. The hunters got back on their horses and went after her.

Reaching the river, Eliza had no time to think. She had to act. She leaped onto the nearest ice cake, and jumped from that to another to another and to another. Sometimes she would lose her footing and fall into the icy water with her child. But she would grasp onto another cake, slide the little girl onto it, and then pull herself up. Wet, shivering with cold, and exhausted, she finally reached the other side of the river, near Ripley. There, a man who had watched with amazement as she had made her way

Eliza Harris and her child are captured in this dramatic portrait cross-ing the Ohio river. With the help of the Underground Railroad they later settled in Canada.

across, took her to a house where he knew fugitive slaves were welcome. It was not considered safe for her to spend the night there, so after she and her little girl had rested, dried their clothes, and eaten, they were taken to an Underground Railroad station a few miles farther from the river.

Her route along the Underground Railroad took her to the home of the Quaker couple, Levi and Catherine Coffin in Newport, Indiana, and it was Catherine Coffin who gave her the name Eliza Harris. From there, she and her daughter continued on to Sandusky, Ohio, where they crossed Lake Erie into Canada.

Some years later the Coffins visited Chatham, Canada, and were delighted to be recognized by Eliza and to learn that she and her daughter were well and happy.

William Wells Brown also received his name from a Quaker who helped him reach freedom. Born in Kentucky in 1814, Brown was probably the youngest of the seven children of Elizabeth, whose master was a Dr. Young. Neither she nor her children had last names. All the children had different fathers. William's father was a white man who asked Dr. Young to promise that he would never sell his son to the slave market in New Orleans. When William was two, Dr. Young moved his family and forty slaves to the Missouri Territory. William grew up on Dr. Young's farm there.

When William was ten or twelve, a son was born

to Dr. Young and his wife. They named him William and decided that their slave William should look after him. But to avoid confusion, they changed the slave William's name to Sandford. There was nothing William or his mother could do about that; a slave had no rights, not even to his name.

In 1827 the Youngs moved to St. Louis and bought another farm. Around that same time, two of Elizabeth's sons died. Three other sons and a daughter worked on the farm, but Elizabeth and William were hired out to various employers in St. Louis. At different times, Brown worked on a steamboat and in a hotel.

While Brown was working at the hotel, Dr. Young experienced some financial difficulties and had to raise money. He sold Elizabeth, her daughter, and three of her sons. Because of his promise to Brown's father, he did not sell Brown but continued hiring him out. The worst job, Brown wrote later, was helping a slave trader and seeing other slave families broken up.

Brown was released from that job probably in the spring of 1833 and returned to Dr. Young, only to learn that he, too, would be sold — not to the Deep South but to a slaveholder in St. Louis. Dr. Young even said he could choose his new owner, but Brown decided to run away and to take his mother, who was still in St. Louis, with him.

One night he stole a rowboat and rowed across the Mississippi River to Illinois. Then he and his

William Wells Brown, a Kentucky born slave, finally made his way north where he settled in Buffalo and wrote one of the first American novels on the black experience.

mother traveled on foot, walking mostly at night and following the North Star, for ten days until they reached Central Illinois, about one hundred fifty miles from St. Louis. They thought they were safe then, and a farm family that fed them and let them spend the night assured them they were. They continued on their journey to Canada traveling by day. As Brown later wrote, "I had just been telling mother how I should try to get employment as soon as we reached Canada, and how I intended to purchase us a little farm, and how I would earn money enough to buy sister and brothers, and how happy we would be in our OWN FREE HOME, — when three men came up on horseback, and ordered us to stop."

The men had a warrant for their arrest as fugitives. They also had a flier advertising them as runaways and offering a reward of two hundred dollars for their return to St. Louis.

The usual punishment for runaways was to sell them to the New Orleans slave market, but Dr. Young continued to keep his promise to Brown's father. Instead, Dr. Young sent him to work in the fields and told the overseer to be hard on him. Elizabeth was not so fortunate. Her owner had her put in jail until he could sell her. When Brown learned that his mother had been sold and would soon be taken to New Orleans, he headed for St. Louis. He managed to find out which steamboat she would be on and went on board to say good-bye and to beg her forgiveness for having gotten her into so much trouble. Calmly, she told him, "You have done nothing more or less than your duty." Then her former master arrived and made Brown leave. His mother cried after him, "God be with you!" and that was the last time he ever saw her.

In the fall of 1833, Dr. Young finally broke his promise and sold Brown to a St. Louis merchant. Not long afterward, Brown accompanied his new owner to Cincinnati, Ohio. As soon as he saw his chance, he took off, traveling on foot, at night, again following the North Star. On the fourth day he ran out of food; on the fifth and sixth day he was caught in a freezing rain and came down with a severe cold. He was about halfway between Cincinnati and

Slave catchers with guns and bloodhounds track the trail of runaways.

Cleveland, although he did not know it then. All he knew was that he had to have help. He hid himself by a road until he saw a man who looked as if he might be kind. The man was a Quaker named Wells Brown. He returned that night with a covered wagon and took Brown to his home. Brown spent two weeks there, until he was well enough to travel.

Brown had already dropped the name Sandford and had started calling himself William again. The Quaker Wells Brown told him that free men had first and last names, and in gratitude William took his friend's names as his own, becoming William Wells Brown.

The Underground Railroad was not well-organized in that area at that time, and Brown was on his own

once he left the Quaker home. He was fortunate to
find others who would give him food along the way
to Cleveland, where he found work, got married,
and taught himself to read and write. He never settled in Canada, but moved instead to Buffalo, New
York, where he later enjoyed a distinguished career
as a writer.

Henry Bibb did go to Canada and became an important leader in the black refugee community there.
Bibb was born a slave in Kentucky in 1815 and from
the time he was a small child was hired out by his
master to work for different farmers. He was often
treated cruelly, worked too hard, and not given
enough to eat. He did not see why he had to be a
slave. He later wrote, "I thought of the fishes of the
water, the fowls of the air, the wild beasts of the
forest, all appeared to be free to go where they
pleased, and I was an unhappy slave." By the time
he was eighteen he had decided to run away, by
somehow getting across the Ohio River and after-
wards to Canada.

But then he met Malinda, a slave belonging to a
master in a different county, and fell in love. After
the two were permitted to have a slave marriage,
which guaranteed them no rights at all, Bibb was
allowed to visit Malinda only on Saturday nights.
Bibb was delighted when William Gatewood, Malinda's owner, bought Bibb, too; but his joy soon
turned to pain and anger. Gatewood abused Malinda

Henry Bibb, a fugitive slave from Kentucky, finally reached Canada on his third attempt and later became the founder of Voice of the Fugitive, *an abolitionist newspaper.*

both physically and sexually, and there was nothing Henry could do about it.

Henry and Malinda had a baby girl, Frances, in 1834, and both hated having to leave her alone and crying while they worked in the fields. Finally, Bibb could stand it no longer. In 1837 he decided to make his way to the North, and there earn enough money to return for his family.

Reaching Ohio, he spent the winter working and saving money and then returned to Kentucky in the spring of 1838. But he was caught and sent south. He managed to escape and went back to get his family; but they were being too closely watched. There was nothing he could do but return to Ohio.

Bibb tried again to rescue his wife and Frances,

again was caught, and again was sold to the Deep
South. After several years, he managed to escape
and, with the help of Underground Railroad agents,
reach Canada. But by this time it was 1845, and
Malinda and Frances were gone. He never heard of
them again.

Bibb spent the rest of his life in Canada helping
other fugitives. He organized the Refugee Home Colony, which purchased thirteen hundred acres of land
for the settlement of fugitive slaves. He taught himself to read and write and, in 1854, founded a newspaper, *Voice of the Fugitive*.

Except in a few cases, such as the work of Harriet
Tubman, the Underground Railroad did not operate
in the Deep South, where it was dangerous even to
question slavery, let alone aid fugitive slaves. Escaped slaves had to make their way to the free states
before they could be helped. They did so using some
ingenious methods.

One of the most remarkable stories is that of William and Ellen Craft, a slave husband and wife who
were owned by separate masters and lived on different plantations in Georgia, far from the Underground Railroad network. Undaunted, they hatched
a clever, but dangerous, plan to escape to the North
in the late fall of 1848.

Ellen was so light-complected that she could pass
for white, and so the plan was for her to dress in
men's clothing and play the part of a young planter.
Most men wore beards in those days, and rather than

Dressed in her master's clothes, Ellen Craft disguised herself as a young planter. Aboard a train she escaped with her husband William to Philadelphia.

try to create a fake beard, the Crafts decided that Ellen would pretend to be suffering from a toothache and wear a bandage around her face. Because Ellen could not write, and thus could not register at hotels along the way, they decided that she should have a sling on her right arm. In fact, they decided, the "young planter" should be so ill that he had to journey to Philadelphia for medical treatment and that on that journey all his needs would have to be attended to by his faithful slave, a situation that was very common between masters and slaves.

William Craft worked as a mechanic in his free time to earn the money necessary for the trip. The couple secured the proper clothing for a young planter — a fine black suit and cloak, high-heeled boots, and tinted green eyeglasses. When all was ready, they set off on their journey.

On a steamer from Savannah, Georgia, to Charleston, South Carolina, Ellen Craft sat right next to the captain at dinner. William Craft later recalled,

> As my master had one hand in a sling it was my duty to carve his food. But when I went out the captain said, "You have a very attentive boy, sir; but you had better watch him like a hawk when you get to the North. He seems all very well here, but he may act quite differently there. I know several gentlemen who have lost their valuable niggers among d____d cut-throat abolitionists."

In response, Ellen Craft merely nodded, fearing that she might give herself away if she spoke.

After they reached Charleston, they registered at a first-class hotel. As they had planned, William Craft explained that his young master could not write. Slaves were not supposed to be able to write, so Craft simply gave the information required, and the hotel employees wrote it in the registration book. They managed the same arrangement when they registered at a hotel in Richmond, Virginia.

At another point in their journey, William Craft was put on the spot. When he went to the train station in Baltimore to purchase tickets to Philadelphia, he was informed that no slave could be issued a ticket without a written guarantee from his master. William Craft heatedly explained that his young master was in such poor health that he might not reach Philadelphia if they were detained. The ticket master waived the rule about the written guarantee and issued two tickets.

By the time the Crafts arrived in Philadelphia, both were exhausted not only from the physical hardships of the long journey but also from the emotional stress of being in constant danger of discovery. Ellen Craft had to spend several days in bed recuperating from the strain. While they were well taken care of by their friends in Philadelphia, they were afraid to stay there long. The city was known for harboring fugitive slaves, and slave catchers were everywhere. So the Crafts soon moved on to Boston. William Wells Brown, a fugitive himself, took them in hand and saw to it that they had many opportunities to tell their exciting story at anti-slavery meetings.

In 1850, the passage of a new fugitive slave law permitted federal officers to seize fugitives anywhere in the United States. Those officers were to be paid a fee for every runaway they apprehended. Now no escaped slave anywhere in the United States was truly safe. The Crafts left for England. Some time after they arrived there, a rumor started that they were unhappy and wished to return to Georgia and slavery. Ellen Craft put the rumor to rest with her letter to a Brititsh anti-slavery newspaper: "I had much rather starve in England, a free woman, than be a slave for the best man that ever breathed upon the American continent."

Another clever fugitive was Henry Brown, a slave in Richmond, Virginia. After thinking long and hard about different methods of escape, he concluded that ordinary ways of travel were too dangerous. He decided to ship himself to Philadelphia. He found a carpenter, a white man, who was willing to make a crate exactly to his specifications: two feet eight inches deep, two feet wide, and three feet long, and lined with baize, a soft fabric similar to felt. On the top was marked, in large letters, "This side up with care."

When all was ready, Henry Brown climbed into the box and the carpenter nailed it shut and further secured it by putting five hickory hoops around it. From that time until he reached Philadelphia, providing that he wasn't discovered along the way, Brown had only an animal-skin bag of water and a few small biscuits to eat. Knowing he would need fresh air, he had also brought along a small tool for boring holes.

Once the crate was nailed shut, another white man whose help Brown had enlisted, a shoe dealer named James Smith, addressed the crate to Philadelphia and saw to it that a wagon carried it to Adams' Express Office. From there, it was transported to Philadelphia by express workers who handled the crate roughly and paid no attention to the

instructions about which side should be up: Henry
Brown traveled standing on his head for miles.

Twenty-six hours after leaving Richmond, Henry
Brown's box arrived in Philadelphia. The Anti-
Slavery Society there had been alerted to his coming
and made sure the box was directed to its offices.
Once they had the box safely inside, members of the
society held their breath as the five hickory hoops
were cut, and the nails removed from the top of the
box. As soon as the lid was off, Henry Brown rose
up and extended his hand, saying, "How do you do,
gentlemen?"

Aside from tiredness and a few bruises, the main
discomfort of the trip for Brown had been his ina-

Henry "Box" Brown gained fame in Underground Railroad circles for
his escape in a box to Philadelphia from Richmond, Virginia.

bility to go to the bathroom except on himself. He was dripping wet. But he was free.

Once he had recuperated from his journey, Henry Brown went to Boston, where he became active in the Underground Railroad there. He was in great demand to speak at anti-slavery meetings for his story caught the imagination of all who heard it. A popular song was written to celebrate his daring escape, and forever after he was known by the nickname "Box" Brown.

Like Brown, Lear Green was shipped to Philadelphia in a box, a sail-or's chest. Yet she has remained an obscure figure in the annals of Un-derground Railroad history.

10
John Brown,
Fugitive Slave

John Brown (not to be confused with the white abolitionist) was born in Southampton County, Virginia, probably around 1810. Until he escaped to freedom, he was known by the name of Fed. His mother, Nancy, called Nanny, belonged to Betty Moore, and John was raised on Betty Moore's land. His father was named Joe and lived on a neighboring plantation, owned by a master named Benford. John Brown believed that his father's father had been stolen from Africa and belonged to the Ibo tribe. John remembered seeing his father only once, for his master moved, taking his slaves with him, and that broke up the family.

John's mother took another husband, a slave who belonged to a master on a neighboring plantation.

Like Nancy's first marriage, this marriage was not formalized. No slave marriage was. Slaves could not marry in a church or before a magistrate, and slave marriages were not recognized by the church or by law. At any time a slave couple, or a slave family, could be broken up or sold. This happened again to John's family, but not for a number of years.

John Brown and his brothers and sisters and half brothers and sisters lived with their mother in a two-room cabin in the slave quarter on Betty Moore's place. They lived in one room, his mother's niece and her children in another.

When very small, John, along with the other children, was taken care of by Betty Moore, who was in her seventies and who used to give all the children a daily dose of garlic, after which they had to run, so they would "grow likely for market." If they didn't run fast enough, she would whip them.

After Betty Moore died, her estate was divided among her heirs. That meant dividing the slaves into equal lots, and that meant separating John Brown's family. He and his mother and little brother Curtis were placed in one lot; his grandmother and younger brother and sister, who were twins, in another. Brown recalled, "But it was of no use lamenting, and as we were to start early next morning, the few things we had were put together that night, and we completed our preparations for parting for life by kissing one another over and over again, and saying good-bye till some of us little ones fell asleep."

John and his mother were taken to Northampton County, North Carolina, by their new master, James Davis. John later described Davis as very cruel. He spent only eighteen months on the Davis farm. One day a slave trader came by and offered good money for slaves to take to Georgia, where the price of cotton had risen and more slaves were needed to raise more cotton. John was sold to the slave trader.

He was about ten years old, and already he had to suffer a second, sad parting from his family. Years later, he recalled,

> At last we got to the gate, and I turned round to see whether I could not get a chance of kissing my mother. She saw me, and made a dart forward to meet me, but Finney [the slave trader] gave me a hard push, which sent me spinning through the gate. He then slammed it to and shut it in my mother's face. That was the last time I ever saw her, nor do I know whether she is alive or dead at this hour.

John was transported to Georgia in a slave coffle, a group of slaves chained together. Whenever they stopped near a large town, the slave trader tried to sell off some of the slaves. He sold John to a farmer in Baldwin County, South Carolina, named Thomas Stevens. Stevens operated a distillery, which made whiskey from corn, and John was placed with Uncle Billy, an old slave who ran the distillery. He also

These slaves are being transported to market in a coffle.

worked with a slave named John Glasgow, who chopped wood to feed the fires of the still.

John Glasgow had been born free in England and had shipped out on merchant ships when still a youth. Later, he had married a white Englishwoman, the daughter of a farmer. While his wife had run their small farm, John Glasgow had gone back to sea. He was about twenty-five years old when he left for a trip to Savannah, Georgia. He had promised his wife that it would be his last voyage, that once he returned he would stay and work the farm and help raise their two small children. But John Glasgow had not realized that in Savannah, Georgia — slave country — even a free man was not free if his skin was black. He was put in jail for the time the ship was in port. The ship was in Savannah a long time, trying to find a cargo, and by the time it was ready to sail the jail fees to be paid to release John Glasgow were so high that the ship's captain refused to pay them. The ship sailed off, and John Glasgow was sold into slavery, winding up the property of Thomas Stevens in South Carolina.

John Glasgow tried to be a father to ten-year-old John Brown. As Brown described later, he was advised by Glasgow "not to cry after my father and mother, and relatives, for I should never see them any more. He encouraged me to try and forget them, for my own sake, and to do what I was bidden. He said I must try, too, to be honest and upright, and if I could ever get to England, where he came from, and conducted myself properly, folks would respect me as much as they did the white man."

Stevens was a cruel master. Brown was whipped over the slightest infraction. Once, after Stevens decided John wasn't ploughing well, he kicked him in the head so hard that he broke John's nose and displaced his right eye. His vision was permanently damaged. After fourteen miserable years, Stevens became ill. A Dr. Hamilton was called in and cured him. Stevens was so grateful that he said he would grant the doctor any favor he asked. The doctor asked for the loan of John Brown, on whom he proceeded to do experiments to see how best to treat sunstroke. In one experiment, a pit was dug in the ground and a fire built in it. After the fire was put

The rod was seldom spared in the daily life of southern plantations and in the homes of northern slaveowners.

out, John was given some sort of medicine and told to strip naked and climb into the pit, with only his head sticking out. Wet blankets covered the pit to keep the heat in. The doctor wanted to know which medicine helped him withstand the most heat. After nine months of undergoing such experiments, John was too weak to work in the fields.

The first time John Brown decided to run away, it was with another slave named Buck. But Buck thought better of the idea and turned John in. Stevens had him flogged for running. Not long after that, Stevens died, and his property was turned over to his son, DeCator, who turned out to be even more cruel than his father. On the death of the elder Stevens, John Glasgow had been given to another son, and John Brown sorely missed the only friend he had. He began to think more and more about England and became determined to get there.

Slaves were allowed to travel alone, if they had a pass from their master. John obtained a forged pass from an old white man in exchange for a hen, and set out for England, although he had no idea where it was. He got as far as Tennessee before someone asked to see his pass and, realizing it was forged, had him put in jail. Rather than be sent back to his master, John escaped and returned to Georgia himself, hoping his only punishment would be a whipping.

But he soon tried to run away again, and this time DeCator Stevens had his head fitted with a peculiar

A slave pass, like this one signed by Jefferson Davis, was needed whenever slaves traveled beyond the confines of a plantation to perform an errand.

metal headdress with bells and horns. John wore that
contraption for three months. Only when it was necessary to remove it so John could work in a corncrib
did it come off. He took that opportunity to escape
again.

Having heard that England was "just across the
water," he thought it was down the Tennessee River
somewhere near New Orleans. He made a raft and
floated down the river, traveling only at night, hiding during the day, stealing potatoes from nearby
fields to eat. He finally reached the Ohio River and
soon after arrived at Paducah, Kansas, and decided
to look for a barbershop, since most barbers in the
United States in those days were blacks. He found
a barber, who fed him and put him up for the night.

Brown then continued on his journey to New Orleans. Once there, he learned that England was half
a continent, plus an ocean, away. In despair, he
allowed himself to be captured and put into a slave
pen, determined to choose his own owner this time.
When shown to prospective masters who looked
mean, he acted sullen, even though the slaves to be
sold were instructed to "look bright." Years later,
Brown explained,

> When spoken to, they must reply quickly, with
> a smile on their lips, though agony is in their
> heart, and the fear trembling in their eye. They
> must answer every question, and do as they are
> bid, to show themselves off; dance, jump, walk,

leap, squat, tumble, and twist about, that the buyer may see they have no stiff joints, or other physical defect. Here may be seen husbands separated from their wives, only by the width of the room, and children from their parents, one or both, witnessing the driving of the bargain that is to tear them asunder forever, yet not a word of lamentation or anguish must escape from them; nor when the deed is consummated, dare they bid one another good-bye, or take one last embrace. Even the poor, dear, little children, who are crying and wringing their hands after 'daddy and mammy,' are not allowed to exchange with them a parting caress. Nature, however, will not be thus controlled, and in

The Society of Friends, better known as the Quakers, and other religious groups played a key role in assisting runaways along the Underground Railroad.

spite of the terrors of the paddle and the cow-
hide, the most fearful scenes of anguish and
confusion often take place, converting the
auction-room into a perfect Bedlam of despair.

Now known as Benford, Brown learned from another slave that if he followed the Mississippi River,
which he would know because it was always muddy,
and went upstream, he would reach Missouri. So
Brown determined to find a buyer from up the Mississippi. When he learned that one Jepsey James was
from up the Mississippi, Brown "looked bright" for
him, even though he thought James looked cruel.
Sold for twelve hundred dollars, John was soon on
his way northward with a coffle of other slaves James
had bought.

James was another cruel master, who ordered preg-
nant women beaten. A hole would be dug for their
bellies, so as not to injure the baby inside them.
Within three months, Brown had run away, following the muddy waters of the Mississippi upstream,
sleeping during the day and walking at night, eating raw corn, potatoes, pine roots, and sassafras
buds.

Arriving in St. Louis, Missouri, on a Sunday
morning Brown sought out a Negro church, where
a deacon fed him and gave him a clean hat and shirt.
Continuing up the Mississippi River, he met a free
Negro who gave him precise directions: "He advised
me not to make for Chicago; to avoid Springfield,

and to go to Indianapolis by way of Vandalia. He
also directed me to call at a place, the name of which,
I think, is Rockville, where I should find a coloured
man, a friend of his, from North Carolina, on whose
aid I might rely." From the North Carolinian, he
obtained another free pass, and with it assumed the
name John Brown.

Continuing on his way, Brown spent time at a
settlement of free black people near Terre Haute,
Indiana. He arrived in Indianapolis to find posters
advertising him as a fugitive and offering a large
reward for his capture. He could not read them,
but a black man whom he met read them for him.
This man told him he had to get out of that
area:

A great many runaways had been traced to that
neighbourhood, which was all in a commotion
in consequence. He added that the Quakers
were known to have helped off the runaways,
by the Underground Railroad, and that they
had been brought into great trouble through it,
and through having otherwise protected coloured people. Numbers of them, he said, had
been ruined by law-suits, which the slaveholders had brought against them; others had
had their farmhouses burnt down, their woods
and plantations set on fire, their crops destroyed, their stock driven off; and many of
them had been themselves seriously injured by

A scene from the slave quarters on a South Carolina plantation.

the violence of mobs. Still, they kept on helping as many slaves as ever, because they felt it to be their duty to do so, and nothing would turn them from it.

John Brown had never heard of the Underground Railroad. The man told him about it. He then gave him directions to a town on the Blue River thirty miles away where a "stationmaster" lived. When Brown reached this free black man's home, he estimated, nine or ten months had gone by since he had run away from DeCator Stevens.

The free black man in turn took Brown to the home of Quakers, who welcomed him as "Friend," let him eat until they worried that he might make himself sick, and put him to bed. He awoke in the middle of the night and was frightened to find himself in a strange place. He recalled many years later,

It was a clear, starlight night, and I could see the walls of the room, and the curtains all of a dazzling whiteness around me. I felt so singularly happy, however, notwithstanding the fear I was in, at not being able to make out where I was, that I could only conclude I was in a dream, or a vision, and for some minutes I could not rid my mind of this idea. At last I became alive to the truth; that I was in a friend's house and that I really was free and safe. I had never learnt to pray; but if what passed in my heart that night was not prayer, I am sure I shall never pray as long as I live.

After several days at this Quaker home, Brown was taken to the house of another Quaker, who took him by wagon a long way (Brown estimated a hundred miles). After several more stops at Underground Railroad stations, Brown reached Detroit, Michigan, where he was introduced to an Englishman who headed a group of English miners on their way to Canada. With this group, he finally reached Canada. It was early in 1849, and John Brown was around forty years old.

In Canada, Brown made his way to the area of Dresden, in Ontario (at that time called Canada

West) where the Dawn Institute was located. Organized in 1842 by Josiah Henson and others as a refuge and training school for fugitive slaves, the Dawn Institute was one of several such refuges in Canadian communities along the Michigan border. There John Brown worked in a sawmill for about six months.

But he had never forgotten his dream of going to England, where his old friend John Glasgow had been born. In July 1850, using money he had earned at the Dawn Institute, he booked passage on the *Parliament* bound for Liverpool. From Liverpool, he made his way to London, where he and his story were celebrated by the British and Foreign Anti-Slavery Society. Alexis Chamerovzow, Secretary of the Anti-Slavery Society, interviewed Brown extensively, and in 1855 published Brown's story, *Slave Life in Georgia: A Narrative of the Life, Sufferings, and Escape of John Brown, Fugitive Slave Now in England*. It joined a growing body of "slave narratives," published both in England and in the United States.

11
The Publicists

It is an interesting coincidence that the term Underground Railroad was first used in the early 1830s, a time when the movement to abolish slavery was growing. There had always been abolitionist sentiment in the country, even before the creation of the United States. The first abolition society was formed in Philadelphia in 1775, the year before the Declaration of Independence. But after the creation of the United States, political events brought the issue of slavery to the forefront of the public mind and caused those who were against it to demand its end.

Slavery was a constant sticking point in relations first between northern and southern colonies and then between northern and southern states. As new states were admitted to the Union, the fight was whether they should be slave states or free. In 1817, Mississippi was admitted to the Union as a slave state, and New York passed a law ordering the gradual but complete abolition of slavery. In 1820, under the Missouri Compromise, Missouri entered the Union as a slave state and Maine as a free state. The United States was then made up of twenty-four states, half slave and half free. But abolitionists were not content with that arrangement. Inspired by the great religious revival that swept the country in the early part of the century, with its moral urgency to end sinful practices and its vision of human perfection, abolitionists believed that slavery was a moral evil and had to be wiped out.

The New England Anti-Slavery Society was formed in 1831 by William Lloyd Garrison and eleven other whites at the African Baptist Church on Boston's Beacon Hill. Earlier the same year Garrison had started his anti-slavery newspaper, *The Liberator*, but while blacks made up the majority of subscribers to the paper they were not invited to participate in the founding of Garrison's organization. Two years later, in 1833, the American Anti-Slavery Society was organized in Philadelphia. Three blacks were among the founders and the sixty-two signers of the society's Declaration of Sentiments.

Margaretta Forten, daughter of James Forten, a wealthy and influential black Philadelphian who was

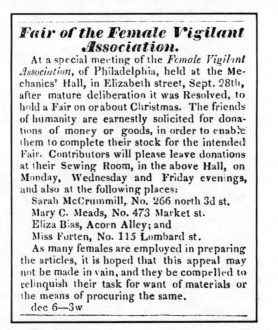

Fair of the Female Vigilant Association.

At a special meeting of the *Female Vigilant Association,* of Philadelphia, held at the Mechanics' Hall, in Elizabeth street, Sept. 28th, after mature deliberation it was Resolved, to hold a Fair on or about Christmas. The friends of humanity are earnestly solicited for donations of money or goods, in order to enable them to complete their stock for the intended Fair. Contributors will please leave donations at their Sewing Room, in the above Hall, on Monday, Wednesday and Friday evenings, and also at the following places:

Sarah McCrummill, No. 266 north 3d st.
Mary C. Meads, No. 473 Market st.
Eliza Bias, Acorn Alley; and
Miss Forten, No. 115 Lombard st.

As many females are employed in preparing the articles, it is hoped that this appeal may not be made in vain, and they be compelled to relinquish their task for want of materials or the means of procuring the same.
dec 6—3w

Many women formed their own organizations to assist with meeting the basic needs of the runaways.

a veteran of the Revolutionary War and who had made a fortune manufacturing sails, helped to found the Female Anti-Slavery Society in Philadelphia in 1833. At that time, women were not generally welcome in men's organizations.

The mission of these societies was not to help escaped slaves, but to bring about an end to slavery. Still, with increased organization of the abolitionists came greater organization of the Underground Railroad, and a growing awareness of how cruel slavery was.

None could relate the evils of slavery better than those who had lived through it. After a time, the anti-slavery societies made testimonies by former fugitives a regular part of their programs.

The more escaped slaves were encouraged to speak at anti-slavery meetings, the more the general public in the North wanted to hear. In 1842, John A. Collins, general agent of the Massachusetts Anti-Slavery Society, wrote to William Lloyd Garrison, "The public have itching ears to hear a colored man speak, and particularly a *slave*. Multitudes will flock to hear one of his class."

The many slave narratives were also powerful weapons against slavery. Usually written by whites because the former slaves themselves could neither read nor write, they were testimonies of the former slaves' lives under slavery and included how they escaped. Frederick Douglass wrote his own and made that clear by titling his first narrative, published in 1845, *Narrative of the Life of Frederick Douglass, An American Slave, Written by Himself*.

Whether written or dictated by the former slaves, these narratives were powerful testimonies to the evils of slavery. A reviewer of Henry Bibb's narrative wrote in 1849 that "This fugitive slave literature is destined to be a powerful lever . . . narratives of slaves go right to the hearts of men."

Not only were the slave narratives powerful, they were also popular. Frederick Douglass's first narrative, published in 1845, sold 5,000 copies in the first four months of publication and 11,000 copies in two years; in Great Britain, nine editions were printed in two years. William Wells Brown's book, also written by himself, went through four editions in its first year of publication.

Although the narrators of these books mentioned that when they were fugitives, they were able to reach freedom with the help of other people, they either did not go into detail or tried to protect those people by changing their names or disguising the places where they lived. After all, the Underground Railroad was an illegal operation, and the people who had been of help might get into trouble if their part were told. As Frederick Douglass wrote in his 1855 autobiography,

> . . . I should frankly state, in advance, my intention to withhold a part of the facts connected with my escape from slavery. There are reasons for this suppression, which I trust the readers will deem altogether valid. It may be easily conceived that a full and complete statement of all the facts pertaining to the flight of a bondman, might implicate and embarrass some who may have . . . assisted him; and no one can wish me to involve any man or woman who has befriended me, even in the liability of embarrassment or trouble . . .

Perhaps that is one reason why the most popular book about fugitive slaves was fiction, although it was based on real-life people, for it went into great

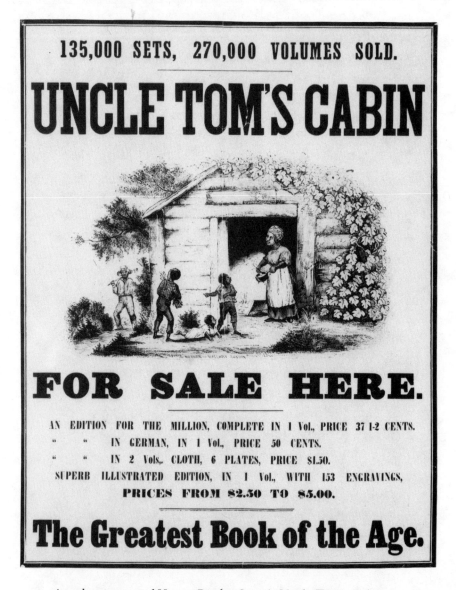

An *advertisement* of Harriet Beecher Stowe's Uncle Tom's Cabin, *a novel depicting plantation life, which placed second to the Bible in the number of copies sold.*

detail about the workings of the Underground Railroad. It was written by a white woman named Harriet Beecher Stowe and was titled *Uncle Tom's Cabin*.

Stowe, who once described herself in a letter as "a little bit of a woman — somewhat more than forty, about as thin and dry as a pinch of snuff; never very much to look at in my best days, and looking like a used-up article now," was born in Litchfield, Connecticut, in 1811. Her father, Lyman Beecher, was pastor of the town's local Congregational Church. When he moved to Cincinnati, Ohio, to head the Lane Theological Seminary in 1832, twenty-one-year-old Harriet, who had been educated as a teacher, went with him. Four years later, in 1836, she married Calvin Ellis Stowe, a professor at the seminary. He was often in poor health, and to help out with the family finances she began to write articles for local newspapers and even published a book about the Pilgrims.

Cincinnati was a border town, separated only by the Ohio River from slave-holding communities like Covington and Newport, Kentucky. Stowe came into contact with fugitive slaves and even helped one escape during a visit to Kentucky. She also met many pro-slavery and anti-slavery activists. During the eighteen years she spent in Cincinnati, she came to believe that there were good and bad people on both sides of the issue but that slavery was morally wrong. The Stowe home in Walnut Hills was a station on the Underground Railroad. But an event in

A *hidden tunnel used by runaways in the basement of the Harriet Beecher Stowe House in Cincinnati is revealed by George Wilson, a former All-American basketball player, who helped restore the historic site.*

her life that really caused her to understand one of the evils of slavery was the loss of her infant son to a cholera epidemic in 1849. Only then did she personally feel the sufferings of slave mothers who were forcibly separated from their children.

In 1850 Calvin Stowe was offered a professorship at Bowdoin College in Brunswick, Maine, and the family moved there. That same year the Fugitive Slave Act was passed. Abolitionists were furious, and Harriet Beecher Stowe was moved to write about slavery and the Underground Railroad in what she thought would be a short novel to be serialized in the *National Era*, an anti-slavery newspaper in Washington, D.C.

The serialized version of the story, *Uncle Tom's Cabin: or, Life Among the Lowly*, which appeared weekly in the newspaper beginning in 1851, was originally planned to be three or four episodes in length. But readers demanded more of the dramatic tale, and Stowe ended up writing forty-five episodes, which ran over the course of ten months. *Uncle Tom's Cabin* was published in book form in 1852 and became an instant best seller; within two months, 300,000 copies had been sold, and the publisher had to run its printing presses day and night to keep up with the demand. Internationally popular as well, the novel was translated into twenty-three languages.

The story was about good and evil. Uncle Tom, the title character, was a gentle, kindly slave, who was sold to the evil plantation owner Simon Legree. The beautiful slave woman Eliza fled to freedom by leaping from ice floe to ice floe across the half-frozen Ohio River with a baby in her arms. A Quaker couple in Indiana, Simeon and Rachel Halliday, welcomed Eliza as she made her way along the Underground Railroad route to Canada.

The names Uncle Tom and Simon Legree are still used today to stand for particular types of people. "Uncle Tom" means a black person who is considered "too friendly" with whites who are not really his friends. "Simon Legree" means a brutal "slave driver" — usually a boss or a husband. Few Americans in the late nineteenth century were not touched by Stowe's book, for it was dramatized and was a standard offering in minstrel and opera house shows.

That is, it was in the free states, where people accepted Stowe's point that slavery destroyed families. People in the slave states called Harriet Beecher Stowe "fanatical" and "bad" and treated her book like poison.

Stowe had expected such criticism and was prepared to deal with it. What made her furious, however, were charges made mostly by southerners that she had portrayed slavery as much more evil than it really was. Most masters were kind and most slaves were happy in slavery, went the southern view. In response, Stowe published her *Key to Uncle Tom's Cabin* in 1853. In it, she cited many proofs that slavery was just as evil, if not more evil, than she had depicted it. But she could not identify the real-life people on whom her characters were based, for that would have put them in too much danger.

Scholars have identified several likely real-life models for characters in Stowe's novel. The character of Uncle Tom was most likely based on Josiah Henson, and even Henson himself came to believe this was true.

Stowe's characters Simeon and Rachel Halliday, who operated an Underground Railroad station in Indiana, were based on the Quaker couple Levi and Catherine Coffin. They really did help a young slave woman who had crossed the ice-filled Ohio River

Levi and Catherine Coffin, a Quaker couple, whose home in Fountain City, Indiana, became a place of refuge for many "passengers" who later made their way to Canada.

with her child in her arms. She was the woman to whom Catherine Coffin gave the name Eliza Harris.

But nothing presented by Stowe could change the minds of pro-slavery people. Even having a copy of Stowe's book could be a crime, which was what happened to a free Negro in Maryland named Sam Green.

Green was suspected of aiding fugitive slaves, and one night in April 1857 a search was made of his home. The search party found a copy of *Uncle Tom's Cabin*, abolition pamphlets, and a map of Canada. He was arrested for possession of the copy of *Uncle Tom's Cabin*, and in May he was found guilty of "having in his possession abolition pamphlets, among which was *Uncle Tom's Cabin*, . . . and sentenced to the penitentiary for the term of ten years — until the 14th of May 1867."

Uncle Tom's Cabin helped the abolitionist cause. It did not do much for the men and women who remained in slavery and still dreamed of escaping. The same was true of the articles, mostly in abolitionist journals, about the successes of the Underground Railroad. Frederick Douglass angrily denounced the writers of these articles in his 1855 autobiography, *My Bondage and My Freedom*. He charged that by writing so openly about it, they had made it "The *Upper*-ground Railroad," and that its stations were "far better known to the slaveholders than to the slaves."

He went on to say:

I honor these good men and women for their noble daring, in willingly subjecting themselves to persecution, by openly avowing their participation in the escape of slaves . . . Nothing is more evident, than that such disclosures are a positive evil to the slaves remaining, and seeking to escape. In publishing such accounts, the anti-slavery man addresses the slaveholder, *not the slave*; he stimulates the former to greater watchfulness, and adds to his facilities for capturing his slave.

Both anti-slavery and pro-slavery forces publicized the Underground Railroad for their own purposes.

Abolitionists used it to dramatize the evils of slavery. Southern slaveholders used it as evidence that northerners were breaking the federal fugitive slave laws. The result was an exaggerated Underground Railroad legend that played up the extent of its organization and the efforts of whites, especially Quakers, and played down the less organized efforts of slaves, free blacks, and other whites.

12
End of the Line

The question of slavery had threatened to split the nation for years. Conflict over it had led the framers of the United States Constitution to write that entire document without once mentioning the words *slave* or *slavery*. That was a compromise between those who were against it and those who were for it.

As time went on, the question continued to be a serious issue of contention between the free states and the slave states. As mentioned earlier, every time a new state was admitted to the Union, there were arguments about whether it should be slave or free. Southern congressmen wouldn't vote to admit a free state unless a slave state was also admitted, for balance. The same was true of northern congressmen.

This balancing act led to some strange compromises, including the so-called Three-Fifths Compromise, in which the issue was representation in Congress based on state population. Only free, white males could vote, and non-slave states had larger white populations. Many slave states had larger slave populations. Under the compromise, for purposes of representation, a slave was deemed to be three-fifths of a man.

By 1850, the issue of slavery was so contentious that another compromise was in order. So many fugitive slaves were being helped to reach Canada that the slaveholding states insisted on yet another law. The free states were against such a law, but were willing to allow it in return for what they wanted — that California be admitted to the Union as a free state. The two sides each gave in a little in order to get their way. The result was the Compromise of 1850. Under it, California was admitted to the Union as a free state; other territories were organized without mention of slavery; and a new fugitive slave law was passed. The Fugitive Slave Law of 1850, besides giving federal officers the power to bring back fugitives and providing for fees to be paid them, also decreed that anyone helping fugitives could be arrested and fined so heavily that they would lose everything they owned.

The enactment of the Fugitive Slave Law resulted in the return of many runaways to the auction block. Even free blacks without identification became victims of this unjust code.

Many southern states were not happy with the Compromise of 1850 and threatened to secede from the Union. They said they would not remain in the Union unless there was strict enforcement of the new Fugitive Slave Law. Slaveholders were determined to find every slave who had escaped and was still living in the United States, even those who had lived as free men and women for years. Some became spies in the North in order to find out information about fugitives.

One Kentucky slave owner disguised himself as a Quaker and went into Indiana to get information about the Underground Railroad. But he was soon found out. Another slaveholder traveled through Indiana and Ohio posing as an anti-slavery lecturer.

Whenever he learned of a fugitive slave in hiding, he notified the master, who then tried to claim his property.

In response to the acts of the slaveholders, and to the new federal law, abolitionists became even more determined to defy the law and help fugitive slaves. On many occasions, groups of anti-slavery people stormed northern jails and courtrooms in order to rescue fugitives who were being held until their fate could be decided. They were often aided by the state and local governments. The free states maintained their right to control what happened within their own borders, and insisted that their laws guaranteeing fugitive slaves certain rights outweighed any federal laws to the contrary.

Then, in 1854, the Kansas-Nebraska Act was passed. Introduced into Congress by Stephen Douglas of Illinois, the act provided that Kansas and Nebraska should be organized as territories and that their territorial legislatures should decide on the question of slavery. Although Kansas did not have a climate that would support large plantations, and thus slavery, pro- and anti-slavery forces struggled over control of the territorial government as if it were a political football.

Abolitionists in several political parties, including the Whigs, Democrats, and Free Soilers, decided to join forces and form a new party that was absolutely against slavery. The Republican Party was born. There had been earlier anti-slavery political parties,

but none of them had attracted a broad base of support. The Republican Party worked hard to do so,
and succeeded.

In the meantime, the United States Supreme
Court handed down a decision that caused pro-
slavery forces to rejoice and anti-slavery forces to
become even more determined to abolish slavery.
The case of *Scott v. Sandford* concerned one Dred
Scott, a Missouri slave whose master had taken him
to live first in free Illinois and then in the northern
part of the Louisiana Purchase, where slavery had
been excluded under the Missouri Compromise of
1820. After Scott was taken back to Missouri, he
sued his master. Scott claimed that living on free
soil had made him free. The majority of the Supreme

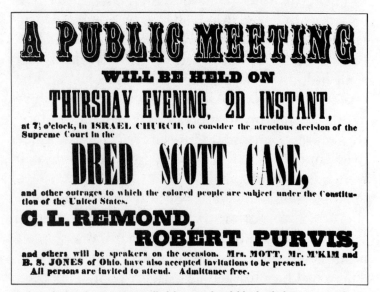

*A broadside of a meeting called by two local black abolitionists to dis-
cuss the landmark Supreme Court Case of Dred Scott.*

Court justices held in 1857 that Scott was not a citizen and thus had no right to bring suit in the courts.

Abolitionists were shocked by this decision. Harriet Beecher Stowe wrote a second novel about the cruelties of slavery, entitled *Dred*, but it was not the best seller that *Uncle Tom's Cabin* had been. To antislavery people, including the new Republican Party, it was clear that they had to gain control of the presidency and the Congress. If they could do so, they might be able to pass an amendment to the Constitution outlawing slavery. The Supreme Court justices, no matter what their personal feelings, would have to uphold the Constitution.

Frederick Douglass wrote that the Supreme Court was not "the only power in this world," and went on to say, "We, the abolitionists and colored people, should meet this decision, unlooked for and monstrous as it appears, in a cheerful spirit. This very attempt to blot out forever the hopes of an enslaved people may be one necessary link in the chain of events preparatory to the complete overthrow of the whole slave system."

In the fall of 1859, the white abolitionist John Brown and a group of followers put into action Brown's plan to liberate a large group of slaves in Virginia. The first step was to raid a federal arsenal and seize guns and ammunition necessary to engage in battle with the slaveholders. They did not have an opportunity to carry out their plan, for the raid on the arsenal was put down by federal troops. In early December, Brown was hanged.

To abolitionists, Brown was a martyr who had died for a just cause. To those who supported slavery, he was an example of the madness of abolitionism. His action, and his execution, caused people who had not yet taken sides to do so. By the time of the presidential election of 1860, there didn't seem to be any compromises left to be made. Those who believed slavery should be abolished went to the polls in 1860 and voted Republican. Abraham Lincoln was elected president.

Although Lincoln was not an active abolitionist, and in fact had mixed feelings about slavery, the South viewed the election of a Republican as a final

Harriet Tubman (far left) and husband Nelson Davis (third from left), a Civil War veteran, are pictured with a group of former slaves she helped escape to freedom.

insult. Events went rapidly downhill.

That December, Harriet Tubman arrived with a group of slaves in Philadelphia and then went to Auburn, New York, to visit her parents. There was so much unrest, and pro-slavery forces were so bitter, that her friends feared for her safety and hurried her off to Canada.

That same month, South Carolina seceded from the Union, soon followed by Alabama, Florida, Georgia, Louisiana, Mississippi, and Texas. By the time the new president arrived in Washington, D.C., to assume the duties of office in late February 1861, the United States included seven fewer states than when he had been elected.

The secessionist states formed a new union called the Confederate States of America. On April 14, Confederate forces seized Fort Sumter in South Carolina, and the Civil War began.

After war broke out, it was not safe even for Harriet Tubman to venture into the South to rescue slaves. So she served the Union cause by working as a scout, a spy, and a nurse for the Union forces. Her work as a nurse was with escaped slaves who managed to reach Union lines sick and starving. Thousands of slaves escaped to Union lines during the war. Eventually, some were allowed to serve with the Union forces.

The Underground Railroad in the North continued to operate as best its agents could manage, for slavery continued in the South, and in fact slaves

The Underground Railroad witnessed its last passengers as slaves traveled with Union troops across state lines, and a new day of opportunity dawned for African Americans.

were forced to work and serve in the Confederate cause. Lincoln's Emancipation Proclamation, under which slavery was abolished in the Confederate States as of January 1, 1863, was of course not obeyed by the Confederacy.

Only after Confederate General Robert E. Lee surrendered to Union General Ulysses S. Grant at Appomattox, Virginia, on April 9, 1865, did slavery take to its deathbed. And only after the Thirteenth Amendment to the Constitution, which officially ended slavery, was ratified in December 1865, did the Underground Railroad come to an end.

But the legend of the Underground Railroad was just beginning. Many agents wrote their reminiscences, or memoirs, of their work on the railroad. William Still, the long-serving member of the Philadelphia Vigilance Committee, had kept secret records over the years of all the many fugitives who had passed through that city; in 1872 he published them in his book, *Underground Railroad Records.*

Many former stations became landmarks. In Ontario, Canada, Josiah Henson's cabin and grave became tourist attractions, and the nearby town of Dresden advertised itself as the Home of Uncle Tom. After Harriet Tubman died, the town of Auburn, New York, placed a tablet at the front entrance of the town courthouse in her honor. It quoted one of her famous sayings, in dialect: "On my Underground Railroad I nebber run my train off de track an' I nebber los' a passenger."

Tubman was a living legend for many years after slavery was ended, for she was only forty-five years old when the Thirteenth Amendment was ratified. She tried but failed to get the government to pay her a pension for her service to the Union forces during the war. So she supported herself by selling eggs and vegetables door-to-door and on the proceeds from her story, *Scenes from the Life of Harriet Tubman*. A neighbor named Sarah Hopkins Bradford wrote the book, for Tubman had never learned to read and write.

In March 1869, Harriet married a young man named Nelson Davis, who was more than twenty years younger than she and suffered from tuberculosis, which he had contracted during the war. Tubman cared for him until he died in 1888 at the age of forty-four. As his widow, Harriet Tubman became eligible to collect twenty dollars a month in military pension. She died on March 10, 1913, having outlived the Underground Railroad by half a century.

Time Line

1518
African slave trade in the New World begins when the first cargo of slaves from Africa arrives in the West Indies

1619
First slaves arrive in Virginia

1600s
In the middle of the century, the Society of Friends, later called Quakers, is founded in England

1770
First American killed in the Revolutionary

cause is a fugitive slave named Crispus Attucks

1775
First abolition society formed in Philadelphia

1786
General George Washington complains that a society of Quakers has attempted to help one of his slaves escape

1787
At the Constitutional Convention in Philadelphia, the "fugitive slave and felon clause" giving slave owners a legal basis for retrieving fugitives is introduced; it becomes Article IV, clause 2, of the United States Constitution

Also in Philadelphia, Quaker Isaac T. Hopper organizes a system for aiding escaped slaves

1793
Fugitive Slave Act passed by Congress

1807
African slave trade abolished in England

1808
Trading in slaves direct from Africa abolished in the United States

1820

Under the Missouri Compromise, Missouri enters the Union as a slave state, Maine as a free state

1826

United States Secretary of State Henry Clay asks Canada for help returning slaves who have escaped there; the Canadian government refuses

1830

First successful run of a steam-powered locomotive

1831

The term "underground railroad" coined (at least in Kentucky and Ohio) when a slave named Tice Davids runs away from his master in Kentucky and disappears in the free state of Ohio

1831

New England Anti-Slavery Society founded by William Lloyd Garrison

1833

Female Anti-Slavery Society formed in Philadelphia by Margaretta Forten and others

1830s
Vigilance committees are formed in many
   northern cities to prevent fugitive slaves
   from being seized and returned to slavery

1839
African slaves revolt on the Spanish ship
   Amistad bound for Cuba. Arriving on
   United States shores, the slaves are al-
   lowed to go free and eventually return to
   Africa

1840s
The term "underground railroad" first appears
   in print

Many northern states pass personal liberty
   laws barring state authorities from helping
   recapture fugitives

1842
In the case of *Prigg v. Pennsylvania*, the
   United States Supreme Court upholds the
   Fugitive Slave Act of 1793 but also holds
   that seizing fugitive slaves is a federal responsibility and that states need not cooperate in any way

1845

Narrative of the Life of Frederick Douglass, an American Slave, Written by Himself published

1850

Fugitive Slave Law passed

1852

Uncle Tom's Cabin by Harriet Beecher Stowe published in book form

1854

Under the Kansas-Nebraska Act, Kansas and Nebraska are organized as territories with the right to decide whether to allow slavery

1857

In *Scott v. Sandford*, the United States Supreme Court rules that blacks, free or slave, are not United States citizens

1850s

The Underground Railroad sees its greatest activity in this decade

1859

On October 16–17, white abolitionist John Brown and twenty-two black and white followers attempt to seize the federal arsenal

at Harpers Ferry, Virginia; the revolt is put
down by federal forces led by Colonel Robert E. Lee

1860

In November, Abraham Lincoln, a Republican, is elected president

In December, South Carolina secedes from
the Union, soon followed by six other
southern states

1861

On April 14, Confederate forces fire on Fort
Sumter in South Carolina and the Civil
War begins

1862

President Lincoln issues the Emancipation
Proclamation, abolishing slavery in the
Confederate states as of January 1, 1863

1865

On April 9, Confederate General Robert E.
Lee surrenders to Union General Ulysses
S. Grant at Appomattox, Virginia

In December, the Thirteenth Amendment to
the United States Constitution, which
outlaws slavery, is ratified

Bibliography

Blockson, Charles L. *The Underground Railroad*. New York: Berkley Books, 1989.

Brown, John. *Slave Life in Georgia: A Narrative of the Life, Sufferings, and Escape of John Brown, a Fugitive Slave*. Savannah, GA: The Beehive Press, 1972.

Buckmaster, Henrietta. *Let My People Go: The Story of the Underground Railroad and the Abolitionist Movement*. Boston: Beacon Press, 1941.

Chang, Ina. *A Separate Battle: Women and the Civil War*. New York: Lodestar, 1991.

Cheek, William F. *Black Resistance Before the Civil War*. Beverly Hills, CA: Glencoe Press, 1970.

Courlander, Harold. *Negro Folk Music U.S.A.* New York: Columbia University Press, 1964.

Davis, Charles T., and Henry Louis Gates, Jr., eds. *The Slave's Narrative.* New York: Oxford University Press, 1985.

Douglass, Frederick. *My Bondage and My Freedom.* New York: Arno Press and *The New York Times,* 1969.

Farrison, William Edward. *William Wells Brown: Author and Reformer.* Chicago: University of Chicago Press, 1969.

Filler, Louis. *The Crusade Against Slavery, 1830– 1860.* New York: Harper & Row, 1960.

Franklin, John Hope, and Alfred A. Moss, Jr. *From Slavery to Freedom: A History of Negro Americans.* Sixth edition. New York: Alfred A. Knopf, 1988.

Harris, Middleton, *et al. The Black Book.* New York: Random House, 1974.

Levine, Ellen. *If You Traveled on the Underground Railroad.* New York: Scholastic Inc., 1988.

Lovell, John, Jr. *Black Song: The Forge and the Flame.* New York: The MacMillan Company, 1972.

McPherson, James M. *Battle Cry of Freedom: The Civil War Era.* New York: Oxford University Press, 1988.

Martin, Waldo E., Jr. *The Mind of Frederick Douglass.* Chapel Hill, NC: University of North Carolina Press, 1984.

Meier, August, and Elliott Rudwich. *From Plantation to Ghetto.* Third edition. New York: Hill & Wang, 1976.

Petry, Ann. *Harriet Tubman: Conductor on the Un-*

derground Railroad. New York: Pocket Books, 1971.

Scott, John Anthony. *Hard Trials on My Way: Slavery and the Struggle Against It, 1800–1860*. New York: Alfred A. Knopf, 1974.

Stampp, Kenneth M. *The Peculiar Institution: Slavery in the Antebellum South*. New York: Vintage Books, 1956.

Winter, Jeannette. *Follow the Drinking Gourd*. New York: Alfred A. Knopf, 1988.

Picture Credits

Index

Italics indicate illustrations

State laws: abolitionists and, 131; slave
catchers and, 78–80
Stationmasters, 21–33; Coffin family,
30–33; Douglass, Frederick, 26, 27,
28, 28, 54, 69; free blacks and, 21–
22, 112; Garrett, Thomas, 29–30,
30, 54, 58; Loguen, Jarmain Wesley,
22, 22, 23–26, 54, 59, 60; numbers
of, 21; Quakers, 28–29, Trowbridge,
Theron, 75
Stations: described, 17–20, 125; loca-
tions of, 15
"Steal Away to Jesus," 67–68
Stevens, Thomas, 103, 105
Still, William, 48, 49, 54, 78, 79, 137
Stowe, Calvin Ellis, 121, 122
Stowe, Harriet Beecher, 120, 121,
122, 122, 123–126, 133

Tallman house (Janesville, Wisconsin),
18
Thirteenth Amendment, U.S. Constitution, 137, 138
Three-Fifths Compromise, 129
Trowbridge, Theron, 75
Tubman, Harriet, 23, 29, 42, 43, 45,
46–56, 57, 58–63, 134, 135; anti-
slavery society and, 60–61; birth of,
43; Brown, John and, 60, 61, 61,
62; childhood of, 43–44; death of,
137–138; finances of, 138; flees from
slavery, 46–48; "Go Down Moses"
and, 66; home of, 59; marriage of,
44; sale of, 44, 46; trips South of,
51–52, 53–56, 59, 62–63, 94
Tubman, John, 44, 51–52

Uncle Tom's Cabin (Stowe), 120
Underground Railroad: Brown, John
(fugitive slave), 101–114; Civil War
and, 135, 136; 137; fiction and, 119,
121, 126–127; Fugitive Slave Act

and, 80; fugitive slaves and, 81–100.
See also Fugitive slaves; maps of, 14–
15; naming of, 1–3; New England
and, 15, 17; organization of, 14;
publicity and, 126–127; Quakers
and, 9, 49, 50–51, 76, 91–92, 109,
111, 112–113; stations described,
17–20, 51, 125; Stowe, Harriet
Beecher and, 121, 122, 122; Uncle
Tom's Cabin (Stowe) and, 123–126;
water transportation, 17
Underground Railroad pass, 28
United States Constitution: fugitive
slaves and, 10–12; slavery and, 128–
129; Thirteenth Amendment to,
137, 138
United States Supreme Court: Amistad
rebellion and, 5; Dred Scott case,
132, 132, 133; Fugitive Slave Act
and, 79–80

Vickers, John, 15
Vigilance committees: Philadelphia
Vigilance Committee, 49, 54, 59,
137; slave catchers and, 78
Voice of the Fugitive (newspaper), 94

"Wade in the Water," 68
Wagons, Underground Railroad and,
19, 19, 20
Washington, George, fugitive slaves
and, 9
Webster, Delia A., 35, 36
Whig party, 131
White, Jane, 39
White, John, 39
Whitson, Thomas, 15, 16
Wilson, George, 122
Windsor, Ontario, Canada, fugitive
slaves in, 55, 55
Women, abolitionism and, 116–117,
117

DATE DUE

STATIONMASTERS AND CONDUCTORS

Jarmain Wesley Loguen

Frederick Douglass

Thomas Garrett

Lydia Hamilton Smith